THE GOSHAWK

THE
GOSHAWK

by

T.H. WHITE

Introduction by Stephen J. Bodio

LYONS & BURFORD, PUBLISHERS

PRINTED IN THE UNITED STATES OF AMERICA

10 9 8 7 6 5 4 3 2 1

LIBRARY OF CONGRESS CATALOGING-IN-PUBLICATION DATA

WHITE, T. H. (TERENCE HANBURY), 1906–1964.
THE GOSHAWK / BY T.H. WHITE.
P.   CM.
ORIGINALLY PUBLISHED: LONDON : CAPE, 1951.
ISBN 1-55821-435-6
1. FALCONRY.   2. GOSHAWK—BIOGRAPHY.   I. TITLE.
SK321.W5   1996
636.6′869′092—DC20
[B]   95-25539
CIP

THIS IS A WILDER PLACES BOOK.
ALL WILDER PLACES BOOKS ARE SELECTED AND INTRODUCED
BY STEPHEN J. BODIO.

THE GOSHAWK

Attilae Hunnorum Regi hominum truculentissimo, qui flagellum Dei dictus fuit, ita placuit Astur, ut in insigni, galea, & pileo eum coronatum gestaret.

ALDROVANDUS

INTRODUCTION

THIS IS a book about excruciatingly bad falconry. It is the best book on falconry, its feel, its emotions, and its flavor, ever written.

In 1936 Terence Hanbury White—always "Tim" to his friends—was between projects. He was thirty years old and had just left his job as the head of the English department at Stowe school to live in a primitive gamekeeper's cottage and write books.

He had some experience. He had written seven novels, all rather light and not too distinguishable today from many other period pieces, but well received. His last book was something different. He had been keeping diaries about his passions—fishing, hunting (on horseback after hounds, the only way English sportsmen allow the word to be used), "shooting" (birds), flying airplanes, and following "miscellaneous" pursuits. This book, *England Have My Bones*, was the first real T. H. White book, where the future creator of Merlin and Wart and Gos began to speak in his own distinctive voice. His biographer, Sylvia Townsend Warner, quotes him as writing to a friend that his previous style was "constipated." But now he had been writing about things he loved, for his own amusement. An early reviewer, James Agate, paid this last book the right compliment, saying, "It is about subjects in which I am not even faintly interested. It is enchanting."

He was at that time the quintessential newly emancipated freelance writer. He was not quite broke—the advance on *England Have My Bones* was good for the time, and the reviews were excellent. But he had expensive tastes, a Bentley convertible (which he had just totaled), the salmon fishing, and shooting and drinking. He was flamboyant, adventurous, often bombastic; also sensitive and, beneath the bluster, terrified. He was often depressed. His £500 advance would not last forever. He "could not make my friends understand that I was working too."

White's stay at the tiny cottage—it had an outhouse, and a well rather than running water—has strange echoes of both Thoreau and the late 1960s. Like Thoreau—and like some back-to-the-landers many years later—he did not need to suffer. His cottage, while simple, was only a half-mile from a road, and cost only 5 shillings a week. He went to the pub every night. The parallels with the '60s are even closer. War loomed on the horizon and White was in an agony about whether it would be best to fight Hitler or to be a pacifist. He feared—as he would again in the nuclear '50s—the breakdown and end of civilization. He wanted to learn survival skills. He also was, in the words of a friend, a "dead serious writer" who wanted to write good books *and* live on them. As he wrote in a moment of despair to his old mentor L. J. Potts, "Writing books is a heartbreaking job. When I write a good one, it is too good for the public and I starve, when a bad one, you and Mary are rude about it."

It was in such a mood that he conceived of a very strange idea. In his wide reading on natural history he had encountered a nineteenth-century text on falconry. In it he read, ". . . a sentence which suddenly struck fire from my mind. The sentence was: 'She reverted to a feral state.' A longing came to my mind that I should be able to do this myself. The word 'feral' has a kind of magical potency which allied itself to two other words, 'ferocious' and 'free.' To revert to a feral state! I took a farm-labourer's cottage and wrote to Germany for a goshawk."

He didn't just want to train a hawk, though he certainly wanted to do that. A writer to the core, he meant to keep a diary and make it into a book. The truest proof of his dedication as both a writer and a falconer is that he never once stopped to ask if anyone wanted to read a modern book on the training of a goshawk.

He started his project in typical headlong White fashion. He was to write later: "I had never trained a serious hawk before, nor met a living falconer, nor seen a hawk that had been trained." He had three books: a "modern" one by Colonel Gilbert Blaine, mostly about peregrines, birds as different from goshawks as dogs are from cats; a nineteenth-century manual from the Badminton Sporting Library, and a copy of Edmund Bert's 1619 treatise on *Hawks and Hawking*. (The last, incidentally, might have done him the most good had he not been constantly reading the books against each other and, worse, second-guessing himself at every frightened, determined step.) But falconry is almost impossible to learn without a human mentor. White didn't have one, so he started alone.

Alone with Gos, that is. White's friend David Garnett later compared *The Goshawk* to a seventeenth-century tale of seduction, or to *The Taming of the Shrew.* "Gos" is every bit as much a character (at one point White refers to him as "a person who was not human") as the narrator is. The very real story—which begins in comedy, approaches tragedy, and is reconciled in knowledge—is the tale of a bungled love affair.

The story unfolds in the past tense, but with a sense of the present so vivid that putting the book down is like waking from a dream. Disaster lurks around every corner. On his second day, Gos escaped in the barn with his leash attached. White knew enough from his reading to know he had made a big mistake; sure enough, the bird ended up hanging by his leash from a nail, "head downward, in rage and terror." White added ingenuously: "Why the leash had not then been tied to a perch, thus preventing his escape, I am not able to remember. Probably I had no perch, and anyway I was in the positions of having to discover all these things by practice." Could it have been his later, less-defensive self who then commented, "It has never been easy to learn life from books"?

He made the same kinds of mistakes throughout the whole affair. If Gos did well, he overfed him. He misjudged the bird's moods and appetite. He overcorrected him and let him get too hungry. Once he hauled the still-leashed hawk down from a tree with a salmon rod, earning its righteous indignation.

Admissions like these drive smug old falconers to fury. They—I mean *we*—all made similar mistakes when we trained our first birds. White presents his earlier self as enthusiastic, furious, terrified, and ignorant, all at the same

4

time. Reading *The Goshawk* can be like reliving a hopeless youthful love affair. You feel each mistake, each stupidity, each irrevocable slip just as you perform it and cannot call it back.

Such heartbreaking and hilarious self-recognition is hardly the only virtue of *The Goshawk*. The book also presents scenes of hallucinatory sleep-deprived beauty (White tried, like a seventeenth-century yeoman, to train the hawk by keeping both of them awake), learned digression, and mock-heroic humor, sometimes all in the same paragraph. Consider this paragraph, in which White tries to call Gos to him on the "creance," a fifty-yard long line, to the tune of "My Lord Is My Shepherd"—and then, when he succeeds, all too typically blows it:

> I put Gos to the railing and retreated to a distance of forty yards, giving ten yards law in order to prevent his being checked in flight, and began to call and whistle. The pursed lips repeatedly proclaimed the Lord their Shepherd, urgently, caressingly, madly, nobly, slowly, rapidly, continuously, with pauses. 'Dinner!' they blew, commandingly, pleadingly, majestically, rapaciously. 'Come along, Gos,' they panderingly, whiningly, peremptorily, softly articulated. 'Now, now,' they remonstrated, feeling rather thankful that this could be done without an audience, 'don't be silly, come-along, be-a-good Gos, Gossy-Gossy-Gos.' And tiddly-tum, tiddly tum, Tiddly Tum Tum repeated echo to whistle, whistle to echo.
>
> For nearly ten minutes the extraordinary uproar went on in the still ridings. So far away that even his flaming eye could no longer be distinguished, the loved goshawk stood

with his back to me, turning his head this way and that. At last he turned upon the perch, roused his feathers into a greedy puff, began to hop upon the railing. The pleas, the tuneless whistling, the staccato notes rose to an orgasm of lust for beef: in vain. They relapsed into the majestic, the quiet, the filled-with-silence pauses. Suddenly, after ten minutes during which he had cocked his head at the creance and visibly pondered its reliability as he moved about, suddenly, and without relation to the pathos of my music, sweet Gos began to fly.

To fly: the horrible aerial toad, the silent-feathered owl, the hump-backed aviating Richard III, he made toward me close to the ground. His wings beat with a measured purpose, the two eyes of his low-held head fixed me with a ghoulish concentration: but like headlamps, like the foreward-fixed eyes of a rower through the air who knew his quay . . . Too frighteningly for words . . . too menacingly he flew, not toward the at-right-angles-held-out beef, but directly toward my face. At five paces nerve broke. I ducked, still holding the beef at the stretch of my arm, and stayed cowering for two beats of the heart.

Gos, of course, sweeps by and must be disentangled from a hedge, where White rewards him for not making a fuss. And so they proceed, from bumble to bungle to curse, weirdly interspersed with Zen-like moments of understanding and calm. ("As I put Gos to bed in the darkness, a new thought emerged. This time it was a quotation: To scorn delights and live laborious days. But it presented itself the other way about, saying: To live laborious days for their delight.")

6

The story of Gos ends in loss; White once again loses him with the leash attached and never sees him again. As Warner puts it, he "felt that book and livelihood were gone too," although he soon got over the feeling and trained a second hawk, Cully, this time succeeding in part because he had learned what mistakes not to make.

He put the book aside. One reason was his embarrassment; one might have been his recognition that Gos's death seemed insignificant with World War II on the horizon. Besides, he was already at work on the book which was to make him famous: *The Sword in the Stone*, the first volume of *The Once and Future King*, which would contain a wonderful scene starring the mad goshawk Colonel Cully. From there, he took his perpetually conflicted conscience to Ireland, where he would sit out the war. It wasn't until well after that, in 1949, when his publisher removed an uncomfortable lump from under a couch cushion and discovered the lost manuscript. He brought a copy back to London and wrote to White that he wanted to publish it. White resisted, but the publisher asked David Garnett to read it and intercede. When Garnett loved it, White agreed, reluctantly. He wrote to this editor, "My shyness about it is personal. You see, apart from not wanting to spread one's personality naked before the public, I have become a much better falconer since then. . . ."

As Warner says, there were indications that his heart might get over it. He wrote a new coda with Cully's first successful hunt, and the book was published, to excellent reviews.

Since then, despite White's misgivings and the discomfort of unreflective falconers, it has wandered in and out of

7

print, one of those books whose fans buy up dozens of copies to give to their friends. Some of its readers are hawk trainers with the insight to see themselves in White, and to see the wisdom of his folly. After all, it was White, not some falconry guru, who realized the hard-earned irreducible core of falconry: "The thing about being associated with a hawk is that you cannot be slipshod about it." Others, readers of nature literature and seekers after serenity, might see that falconry was a metaphor for the difficulty and necessity of real relationships with nature: ". . . because the faculties exercised were those that throve among trees rather than houses, and because the whole thing was inexpressibly difficult."

I read T. H. White's *The Goshawk* and *The Sword in the Stone* years before I ever saw a gos. Thirty-some years later, I have a goshawk in the yard (her name is Sara, she is five years past the tough times, and she comes from the Wind River Range rather than Germany, but her nature is the same as that of Gos) as well as first editions of White's books on my shelf. I still reread *The Goshawk* every year. I don't read it because I am a falconer, or even a goshawker, but because it is one of the best books ever written about a human and an animal, and because it is as fresh and contemporary as though it had been written yesterday. I'll say no more; it's time to join the young Tim White in his barn, by lantern light.

—Stephen Bodio
Bozeman, MT

PART ONE

CHAPTER I

Tuesday

W H E N I first saw him he was a round thing like a clothes basket covered with sacking. But he was tumultuous and frightening, repulsive in the same way as snakes are frightening to people who do not know them, or dangerous as the sudden movement of a toad by the door step when one goes out at night with a lantern into the dew. The sacking had been sewn with string, and he was bumping against it from underneath: bump, bump, bump, incessantly, with more than a hint of lunacy. The basket pulsed like a big heart in fever. It gave out weird cries of protest, hysterical, terrified, but furious and authoritative. It would have eaten anybody alive.

Imagine what his life had been till then. When he was an infant, still unable to fly and untidy with bits of fluff, still that kind of mottled, motive and gaping toad which confronts us when we look into birds' nests in May: when, moreover, he was a citizen of Germany, so far away: a glaring man had come to his mother's nest with a basket like this one, and had stuffed him in. He had never seen a human being, never been confined in such a box, which smelled of darkness and manufacture and the stink of man. It must have been like death — the thing which we can never know beforehand — as, with clumsy talons groping for an unnatural foothold, his fledgeling consciousness was hunched and bundled in the oblong, alien surroundingness. The guttural voices, the un-birdlike den he was taken to, the scaly hands which bound him, the second basket, the smell and noise of the motor car, the unbearable, measured clamour of the aircraft which bounced those skidding talons on the untrustworthy woven floor all the way to England: heat, fear, noise, hunger, the reverse of nature: with these to stomach, terrified, but still nobly and madly defiant, the eyas goshawk had arrived at my small cottage in his accursed basket — a wild and adolescent creature whose father and mother in eagles' nests had fed him with bloody meat still quivering with life, a foreigner from far black pine slopes, where a bundle of precipitous sticks and some white droppings, with a few bones and feathers splashed over the tree foot, had been to him the ancestral heritage. He was born to fly, sloping sideways, free among the verdure of that Teutonic upland, to murder with his fierce feet and to consume with that curved Persian beak, who now hopped up and down in the clothes basket with a kind of imperious precocity, the impatience of a spoiled but noble heir apparent to the Holy Roman Empire.

I picked up the clothes basket in a gingerly way and carried it to the barn. The workman's cottage which I lived in had been built under Queen Victoria, with barn and pigsty and bakehouse, and it had once been inhabited by a gamekeeper. There in the wood, long ago when Englishmen lived their own sports, instead of competing at games with tedious abstract tennis bats and cricket sticks and golfing mallets as they do today, the keeper who lived in the cottage had reared his pheasants. There was no wire netting in his days, and the windows of the low barn were enclosed with wooden slats, nailed criss-cross, a diamond lattice work. I put Gos down in the barn, in his basket, and was splitting a rabbit's head to get at the brain, when two friends whose sad employment I had lately followed came to take me to a public house for the last time. The hawk came out of the basket already strong on the wing, beat up to the rafters, while his master, armed with two pairs of leather gloves on each hand, cowered near the floor — and then there was no more time. I had intended to put a pair of jesses on him at once, but he flew up before I had pulled myself together: and it was only when the great bundle of young feathers was perching on the rafters that one could see the jesses already on him. Jesses were what they called the thongs about his feet. Jessed but not belled, perched at the top of the old gamekeeper's loft, baleful and extraordinary, I left the goshawk to settle down: while we three went out to the public house for a kind of last supper, at which none was more impatient of translation than the departing guest.

They brought me back at about eleven o'clock, and by midnight I had given them drink and wished them fortune. They were good people, so far as their race went, for they were among the few in it who had warm hearts, but I was glad to see them go: glad to shake off with them the last of an old human life, and to turn to the cobwebby outhouse where Gos and a new destiny sat together in contrary arrogance.

The hawk was on the highest rafter, out of reach, looking down with his head on one side and a faint suggestion of Lars Porsena. Humanity could not get there.

Fortunately my human manœuvres disturbed the creature, shook him off the high perch to which he was entitled by nature and unused by practice — unused by the practice which had stormed at him with mechanical noises and shaken him with industrial jolts and bent his tail feathers into a parody of a Woolworth mop.

He flew, stupid with too many experiences, off the perch at which he would have been impregnable. There was sorrow in the inapt evasion. A goshawk, too gigantic for a British species, and only three inches shorter than the golden eagle, was not meant to run away but to run after. The result was that now in this confinement of unknown brick walls, he fled gauchely, round and about the dreary room: until he was caught after a few circuits by the jesses, and I stood, stupefied at such temerity, with the monster on my fist.

Night

The yellowish breast-feathers — Naples Yellow — were streaked downward with long, arrow-shaped hackles of Burnt Umber: his talons, like scimitars, clutched the leather glove on which he stood with a convulsive grip: for an instant he stared upon me with a mad, marigold or dandelion eye, all his plumage flat to the body and his head crouched like a snake's in fear or hatred, then bated wildly from the fist.

Bated. They still said that Jones minor got into a bate that morning, at preparatory schools. It was a word that had been used since falcons were first flown in England, since England was first a country therefore. It meant the headlong dive of rage and terror, by which a leashed hawk leaps from the fist in a wild bid for freedom, and hangs upside down by his jesses in a flurry of pinions like a chicken being decapitated, revolving, struggling, in danger of damaging his primaries.

It was the falconer's duty to lift the hawk back to the fist with his other hand in gentleness and patience, only to have him bate again, once, twice, twenty, fifty times, all night — in the shadowy, midnight barn, by the light of the second-hand paraffin lamp.

It was two years ago.* I had never trained a serious hawk before, nor met a living falconer, nor seen a hawk that had been trained. I had three books. One of them was by Gilbert Blaine, the second

* In 1937.

was a half-volume in the Badminton Library and the third was Bert's *Treatise of Hawks and Hawking*, which had been printed in 1619. From these I had a theoretical idea, and a very out-of-date idea, of the way to man a hawk.

In teaching a hawk it was useless to bludgeon the creature into submission. The raptors had no tradition of masochism, and the more one menaced or tortured them, the more they menaced in return. Wild and intransigent, it was yet necessary to 'break' them somehow or other, before they could be tamed and taught. Any cruelty, being immediately resented, was worse than useless, because the bird would never bend or break to it. He possessed the last inviolable sanctuary of death. The mishandled raptor chose to die.

So the old hawk-masters had invented a means of taming them which offered no visible cruelty, and whose secret cruelty had to be born by the trainer as well as by the bird. They kept the bird awake. Not by nudging it, or by any mechanical means, but by walking about with their pupil on the fist and staying awake themselves. The hawk was 'watched', was deprived of sleep by a sleepless man, day and night, for a space of two, three or as much as nine nights together. It was only the stupid teachers who could go as far as nine nights: the genius could do with two, and the average man with three. All the time he treated his captive with more than every courtesy, more than every kindness and consideration. The captive did not know that it was being kept awake by an act of will, but only that it was awake, and in the end, becoming too sleepy to mind what happened, it would droop its head and wings and go to sleep on the fist. It would say: 'I am so tired that I will accept this curious perch, repose my trust in this curious creature, anything so I may rest.'

This was what I was now setting out to do. I was to stay awake if necessary for three days and nights, during which, I hoped, the tyrant would learn to stop his bating and to accept my hand as a perch, would consent to eat there and would become a little accustomed to the strange life of human beings.

In this there was much interest and joy — the joy of the discoverer — much to think about, and very much to observe. It meant walking round and round in the lamplight, constantly lifting back the sufferer, with a gentle hand under his breast, after the hundredth bate: it meant humming to oneself un-tunefully, talking to the hawk, stroking his talons with a feather when he did consent to stay on the glove: it meant reciting Shakespeare to keep awake, and thinking with pride and happiness about the hawk's tradition.

Falconry was perhaps the oldest sport persisting in the world. There was a bas-relief of a Babylonian with a hawk on his fist in Khorsabad, which dated from 3000 years ago. Many people were not able to understand why this was pleasant, but it was. I thought it was right that I should now be happy to continue as one of a long line. The unconscious of the race was a medium in which one's own unconscious microscopically swam, and not only in that of the living race but of all the races which had gone before. The Assyrian had begotten children. I grasped that ancestor's bony hand, in which all the knuckles were as well defined as the nutty calf of his bas-relief leg, across the centuries.

Hawks were the nobility of the air, ruled by the eagle. They were the only creatures for which man had troubled to legislate. We still passed laws which preserved certain birds or made certain ways of taking them illegal, but we never troubled to lay down rules for the birds themselves. We did not say that a pheasant must only belong to a civil servant or a partridge to an inspector-of-filling-up-forms. But in the old days, when to understand the manage of a falcon was the criterion by which a gentleman could be recognized — and in those days a gentleman was a defined term, so that to be proclaimed 'noe gent.' by a college of arms was equivalent to being proclaimed no airman by the Royal Aero Club or no motorist by the licensing authorities — the *Boke of St. Albans* had laid down precisely the classes of people to whom any proper-minded member of the Falconidae might belong. An eagle for an emperor, a peregrine for an earl: the list had defined itself meticulously downward to the kestrel, and he, as a crowning insult, was allowed to belong to a mere knave — because he was useless to be trained. Well, a goshawk was the proper servant for a yeoman, and I was well content with that.

There were two kinds of these raptors, the long- and the short-winged hawks. Long-winged hawks, whose first primary feather was on the whole the longest, were the 'falcons', who were attended by falconers. Short-winged hawks, whose fourth primary was the longest, were the true 'hawks', who were attended by austringers. Falcons flew high and stooped upon their quarry: hawks flew low, and slew by stealth. Gos was a chieftain among the latter.

But it was his own personality that gave more pleasure than his lineage. He had a way of looking. Cats can watch a mousehole cruelly, dogs can be seen to watch their masters with love, a mouse watched Robert Burns with fear. Gos watched intently. It was an alert, concentrated, piercing look. My duty at present was not to return it. Hawks are sensitive to the eye and do not like to be regarded. It is their prerogative to regard. The tact of the austringer in this matter was now delightful to me. It was necessary to stand still or to walk gently in the mellow light of the barn, staring straight in front. The attitude was to be conciliatory, yielding, patient, but certain of a firm objective. One was to stand, looking past the hawk into the shadows, making minute and cautious movements, with every faculty on the stretch. There was a rabbit's head in the glove, split in order to show the brains. With this I was to stroke the talons, the chest, the entering edge of the wings. If it annoyed him in one way I must desist immediately, even before he was annoyed: if in another, so that he would peck at what annoyed him, I must continue. Slowly, end-lessly, love-givingly, persistently, it was my business to distinguish the annoyances: to stroke and tease the talons, to recite, to make the kindest remonstrances, to flirtingly whistle.

After an hour or two of this, I began to bethink myself. He had already begun to calm down, and would sit on the glove without much bating. But he had suffered a long and terrible journey, so that perhaps it would be better not to 'watch' him (keep him awake) this first night. Perhaps I would let him recuperate a little, free him in the barn, and only come to him at intervals.

It was when I went to him at five minutes past three in the morning, that he stepped voluntary to the fist. Hitherto he had been found in inaccessible places, perched on the highest rafter or flying away from perch to perch. Now, smoothing up to him with stretched hand and imperceptible feet, I was rewarded with a triumph. Gos, with confident but partly dis-dainful gesture, stepped to the out-feeling glove. He began, not only to peck the rabbit, but distantly to feed.

It was at ten past four that we encountered next, and already there was a stirring of the dawn. A just-lighterness of the sky, noticed at once on stepping from the kitchen fire, a coldness in the air and humid-ity underfoot, told that that God who indifferently administers justice had again ordained the miracle. I stepped from the cottage fire to the future air, up earlier even than the birds, and went to my grand captive in his beamed barn. The brighter light shone on his primaries, a steely lustre, and at ten to five the glow in the small two-shilling lamp was vanquished. Outside, in greyness and dim twilight, the very first birds not sang but moved on their perches. An angler who had been sleepless went past in the half mist to tempt the carp of the lake. He stopped outside the lattice, looked in upon us, but was urged to take his way. Gos bore him fairly well.

He was eating now, pettishly, on the fist, and Rome was not built in a day. Rome was the city in which Tarquin ravished Lucrece; and Gos was Roman as well as Teutonic. He was a Tarquin of the meat he tore, and now the man who owned him decided that he had learned enough. He had met a strange fisherman through the dawning window: he had learned to bite at rabbits' legs, though mincingly: and when he was hungrier he would be more humble.

I came away through the deep dew to make myself a cup of tea: then rapturously, from six until half past nine in the morning, I went to sleep.

Wednesday

At ten o'clock on the next day the hawk had not seen humanity for four hours, although he was sharper set. He had probably also been asleep during that time (unless the daylight and uncertainty would have kept him awake), so that, although he was hungry, he was partly liberated from the imposition of a human personality. He would no longer step to the

HAWK FURNITURE

glove, as he had done since three o'clock, but again fled from rafter to rafter as if he were just out of the basket. It was a set-back in the process of success, and it caused a scene.

A hawk was held by a pair of jesses, one on each leg, which were united at the ends remote from the leg by means of a swivel through which the leash could be passed.

One of Gos's jesses being worn out at the swivel hole, it had been impossible to pass the leash (a leather boot lace in my case) through its proper swivel. I could not attach the swivel. For that matter, I still lacked a swivel. So the two jesses had been tied together, and then knotted to a piece of string for leash. Why the leash had not then been tied to a perch, thus preventing his escape, I am not able to remember. Probably I had no perch, and anyway I was in the position of having to discover all these things by practice. It has never been easy to learn life from books.

The upshot was that now, loping away from his tormentor on silent wings, the bird caught his leash on a nail and hung head downward in rage and terror. It was in this mood that we were to begin his first full day, and the curious result of it was that immediately he had been secured he began to eat ravenously, standing square and easy, until he had consumed a whole leg. He was always more amenable after a good fuss, as I found later.

A boy for whom I had once kept two sparrow-hawks, arrived at half after twelve. It had been possible during the still hours to make a careful inventory of the hawk's plumage, and the results were not satisfactory. The tips of all the primary wing feathers were snapped off for about an eighth of an inch, and the whole tail had been skewed sideways by his struggles in the basket, until it was not possible to distinguish any

details in the horrid tangle. The way to straighten out
the tail feathers was to dip them into almost boiling
water for half a minute. It was necessary to decide
whether this ought to be done now or later. If now,
and if with a clumsy and acrimonious scene, it would
mar those first amicable impressions which were said
to be so important in every walk of life. If later, and
also with a scene, it might undo whole weeks of training. I took the bold step and put the saucepan on the
fire. I might as well be hanged for a sheep as a lamb,
I thought, and so I would introduce the boy to the
hawk at the same time. He would be useful in the
subsequent operation.

The first stage in training a hawk was called
'manning' him: and this meant to make him accustomed to man in all his activities, so that he was no
longer frightened. With a falcon, you first accustomed
him to yourself in the dark, later in shaded light, later
by day: finally you brought him to a stranger who had
been instructed to sit quite still without looking at him,
and so on. A goshawk might take about two months,
before he would tolerate motor cars and everything
else. This was the reason why the fisherman's visit
had been an interesting step, why the introduction of
the boy, in full daylight, was now to be a crisis.

The crisis was successful. Thinking about it in
advance, as one had to plot extempore each step in
the training of a hawk, I had kept back the rabbit's
liver, a tit-bit, as a bribe similar to the jam in which
they used to give us powders. I told the boy my plans,

went down to Gos and fed him with half the liver; admitted the boy five minutes later; waited till the hawk had taken stock of him: brought him, on the left hand, three times up to my chest — nearer, nearer, finally touching — and at the fourth time, passing the right hand gently over his back, held him soft but firm in a single movement. Talking to him, holding him compactly so that because he could not struggle he would not afterwards remember it as a struggle, we dipped the tail feathers into the saucepan, changed the worn jess for a new one, substituted a proper leather leash for the piece of string, and pressed Gos gently back on the fist, without an unhappy memory. Immediately, although the boy was there, Gos fell upon the remainder of the liver, and wolfed it as if he had never eaten anywhere but on the glove: square-straddled, grip-taloned, mantling over the bloody morsels, tearing at them like the eagle of Prometheus.

'Isn't he lovely!' said the boy, with awe and reverence, and a proper lust to have one too.

Thursday

A keeper of long-winged hawks used to be called a falconer, of short-winged hawks an austringer. The word was derived from the same root as ostrich, the biggest of birds. The training of the goshawk, the largest European short-winged hawk, might be expected to last about two months. In this time an ungovernable creature would have been taught to do, under government, what it would instinctively have done in two or three days in a free state. Two months was a long time.

What a goshawk learned in one day would rarely be appreciable to anybody but its master, so cautious and delicate was the progress, and the real difficulty of writing a book upon the subject would be to know which detail ought to be left out. I had decided to write a book. In the hawk's day-book every meal was entered, as it happened, with its time and amount, and every step, forward or backward, was noted with the tedium of true love. From this a patient reader would have to be spared. Yet half the interest, if there were any, in a book about falconry, would obviously reside in these very details. Then again, there was the danger of being didactic or too technical, and there was the folly of thinking that anybody would want to buy a book about mere birds — with no film-stresses in it, and no close-up hug in the last chapter. All the same, I had to write a book of some sort, for I only had a hundred pounds in the world and my keeper's cottage cost me five shillings a week. It seemed best to write about what I was interested in.

My intellectual friends of those days, between the wars, used to say to me: 'Why on earth do you waste your talents feeding wild birds with dead rabbits?' Was this a man's work today? They urged that I was an intelligent fellow: I must be serious. 'To arms!' they cried. 'Down with the Fascists, and Long Live the People!' Thus, as we have since seen, everybody was to fly to arms, and shoot the people.

It was useless to tell them that I would rather shoot rabbits than people.

But what on earth was the book to be about? It would be about the efforts of a second-rate philosopher who lived alone in a wood, being tired of most humans in any case, to train a person who was not human, but a bird. These efforts might have some value because they were continually faced with those difficulties which the mind has to circumvent, because falconry was an historic though dying sport, because the faculties exercised were those which throve among trees rather than houses, and because the whole thing was inexpressibly difficult. There were two men I knew of by correspondence, to whom one could turn for advice. They were busy themselves, and might take a fortnight to answer a letter. With the aid of these answers, and of three printed books, I was trying to reconquer a territory over which the contemporaries of Chaucer had rambled free.

Down with the rabbits then, and long live the people. If my readers liked to take a patient excursion into the fields and back into the past, so. And if not, well; at least I would not shoot the ones who did not read me.

Monday, Tuesday, Wednesday

I would have to start with sleep. There must have been many thousands of humans living then who had had no sleep for three days and three nights, on account of the first World War. But the point was that the austringer, since he rode to battle in the train of William, had been accustomed to perform this feat for three nights, every time he acquired a passage hawk. Man against bird, with God for an umpire, they had sat each other out for three thousand years. When the austringer was married or provided with assistants, it had no doubt been easy to cheat in the great match. He would have taken a sea-watch now and then, while another carried on the battle. But when he was a bachelor, when poor and without assistance, he, in his own person, had vanquished the endurance of the king of birds by pitting against it the endurance of a servant of man.

From that Monday morning until four o'clock on the Thursday morning, I had six and a half hours of odd sleep. It was enjoyable. The watching of hawks, the triumph over them (as it were) man against man, the extremely beautiful experiences of night denied to so large a percentage of civilization, the feeling of triumphant endurance which emerged from so many hells in which sleep was lusted for, the weary joy with which the succeeding capitulations of the enemy were noted one after the other, it was these things which, under the heading of their days, I must try to remember.

It would be better to leave them in the jumble to which the greed for sleep reduced them, just bringing to coherence that maze of almost somnambulant entries in the day-book, stragglingly written with one hand while the hawk sat on the other. They were a cry from hell, but of the triumphant and delighted damned. 'If you don't mind the inconvenience of sitting up with him three nights,' said my authority, Gilbert Blaine, 'the falcon may be tamed in three days.' Magnificent meiosis! Unconquerable martyr to the noble science!

There were two places: a small kitchen, with a fire in it and an easy chair, was one, and the other was that lamp-lit barn. The wind came through the cracks in the weather-boarding on one side, went out through the lattice work into the night which the lamp made black. A few sticks, bottles, half bricks, spider's webs and part of a rusty oven adorned the Rembrandt interior. This was the torture chamber, the medieval dungeon in which the robber baron was to be tormented. One felt like an executioner, very much as if the black mask ought to have concealed one's face, as one worked by dim wick-light in solitude amid the shrieks of the victim. Like a hare, like a child in agony, like a crazed captive in horrors of the Bastille, Gos screamed as he bated, hung twisting upside down with yell upon yell. And then, suddenly, there was an owl outside. The screams were answered. 'A moi! A moi! Auita! Hilfe!' And 'Coming! Coming!' cried the owl: 'Be brave, we will help, hold out!' It was eerie, terrifying almost, to stand between the counter-answered shrieks of the martyr and his compatriot, in the dungeon silent and night-stricken.

The day-book holds forgotten pictures. There was the man swaying gently to and fro on his feet, like a

29

pendulum. He held the hawk on one fist and a rabbit's leg in the other, and he was reciting. His eyes were shut, and so were the hawk's. Both were asleep. There was the man counting the diminishing number of bates at each visit: there were the walks along solitary ridings during the day-time, the mental calculations at each advance, the half-hours by the kitchen fire in which pen and whisky tried to keep pace with sleep, the fingers which smarted from pecks, the fetching of coal through the dewy night grass under an enormous orange moon in its last quarter: there were mist, wet boots, silence, solitude, stars, success and obedience.

On the last night everything came to a head. Man's stamina had failed with hawk's, so that now I had convinced myself that he might be watched in the kitchen. It had a tiled floor which his mutes would not stain, a fire, an aladdin lamp, and a chair. My dear bitch Brownie sat on a chair to the right of the fire, myself to the left, and the hawk stood on an improvised perch in the middle. Screaming no longer, but cheeping like a robin, Gos did not know which way to look. As the strong lamp was turned up he watched it closely, for it was magic. The beam rose to the ceiling, and he followed it upward to its circle of light. I turned it up and down to keep him awake, and his head went with the light. Raising his tail, he squirted a jet of mutes across the floor, looked round in tired pride of creation. The hours went and his head drooped, his eyes blinked and sealed. I got up to take him on fist so that he should not sleep: but was stupid with watching also, and fumbled the knots. The wings swept out at the wrong moment, the leash slipped, and the worn-out eagle was sitting on the top of a Sèvres tureen, the only piece of valuable china in the room. The sleep-shotten man collected his wits to face the new crisis. Both were too beaten to give each other trouble. But, just as the hawk was being tied to the perch again, the bitch, as a third party, joined in. Brownie, who had lived as often my sole and always my chief and most beloved companion for two years, had for days and nights been without notice. Her anxious face, watching this incomprehensible desertion, had become more and more pitiful without receiving pity. Suddenly it was too much for her. She came humbly, heart-brokenly, asking with fear and desolation for any re-assurance. Of this new, mad-eyed and absent master she was even afraid, and came up in a way which it would hurt to describe. She said: Am I for always thrown off? So now the man had to pull himself together for a new demand, to comfort the poor creature out of a heart with no energy to spare. Her puzzled and sorrowful face was too much for exhaustion.

When Gos finally gave in, the conquest was a visible one. Sitting on the fist, his head drooped, and his wings mantled. No longer firm and spruce at the shoulders, they hung down on either side of the body, humbly resting their forward edges against the supporting arm. The eyelids irresistibly rose up over the capitulated eyes, the head nodded for the sleep which his master, as tired as he was, was forced by a gentle movement to deny him. Between the two protagonists a link had been established, of pity on the one side and confidence on the other. We had waited patiently for seventy-two hours for this moment; the moment at which the hawk, co-erced by no cruelty of mine but only by the desire for sleep (which he did not connect with me), could first say with confidence: 'I am so sleepy that I will trust this glove as a perch to sleep on, even though you stroke me, even though you have no wings and a beak of pliable gristle.'

Thursday

A solitary and self-supporting austringer had little time in which to live a life of his own, could not, in fact, live at all except in so far as his life was his work. In this respect he resembled the agricultural labourer of the last century. For every holiday which he took away from the hawk, the hawk would go back in its training twice as fast as he could hope to make it go forward. Theoretically he ought to have carried the creature with him wherever he went, from dawn till dark, and ought only to have visited the places which suited the hawk. He was manning it now, introducing it successively to one shock after another. Its excursions were to be planned on this basis, so that it met a stranger standing still, a stranger walking and running, two strangers, children, groups, a bicyclist, a motor car, traffic, and so on. All the time it ought to have lived, and had to eat, on the glove alone. It had got to learn to regard that glove as its natural home and perch, so that, when the great and distant day arrived for flying it free, it would return to the glove automatically, having no life outside it. The quickest way to train a goshawk would have been to get up at six o'clock and to carry the bird about for twelve hours every day, for a month or two, without intermission.* So that even a retainered austringer would have been a busy man.

I got up again at noon, for now the problem of food was becoming pressing. There was not only the ideal of carrying Gos all day, but also the necessity of killing his food and dressing my own. This brings in the next picture, not that of endurance by night nor of the ceaseless daily hardihood implicit in this kind of colonist's existence, but the picture of the weather and the season. Nothing was more woven into the stuff of falconry than the sun and the wind. Being so much out in the open gave a tone to the whole thing, a background to life very different from any local background of tree or house. The same field or hawk was changed in rain, the same circumstances were happy or sorrowful as the sun shone. When I had been about the business for a month or two, farmers would ask me whether it was going to be fine on the morrow in much the same way as one is supposed to ask a mariner. They reposed but little confidence in my judgment, it is true, but occasionally they would take the trouble to ask and to reflect upon the answer; for

* See Postscript.

they knew that my eye was in the sky as much as theirs. I was wrong about as often as they were; which was generally.

So there should be given a picture of the weather as we started. It was at the end of July, and, though the spring and summer had been miserable in England, just then we had a few fine moments. This cast a happy tone over the first days with Gos, so that they remember themselves as days of long walking. In the afternoons mainly I used to go out for his food, for it was preferable that he should be given fresh food every day. There were long tours, very contented to be alone at last, with the gun-barrel warm in the sun: there was the busy life of the summer hedges, with the wide stalks, and the quite untroubled murder of rabbits sitting. One was shooting not in the least for sport, but for the pot, and it was necessary to get back to the hawk as quickly as possible. The necessity of wasting no time and of killing with certainty had a terrible effect upon the shooting, making one poke out of anxiety, and I wondered what would happen when the next World War had reduced us to savagery and hunting for ourselves. The art of shooting flying would fall into abeyance then, with the looted cartridges scarce and the food so precious. When the cartridges had run right out the goshawk would be a real blessing. The French called him *cuisinier*, the caterer for the mess.

Then there was the queerly savage picture of the sun-broiled man, after he had crept upon the rabbit and assassinated it, knocking it quickly on the head, throwing it upon its back, and immediately beginning to draw the sharp blade of his knife across the skin of the stomach. The leisurely gentility with which the shooting man harls the dead body, and slings it over the hasp of a gate as something no longer interesting, were gone. I supposed a concealed watcher would have thought one quite animal again, like an aborigine or a fox, or even like the hawk itself. The sunny picture was first one of creeping movement, split up into sudden activity by the loud bang, the rush, the *coup de grâce*: and then again it was static, a little huddle of small movements mantling over the prey. It was necessary to eviscerate these rabbits as quickly as possible, because it kept them fresh.

It was on this day that I saw what I then thought was a pair of sparrow-hawks. Most shooting people in England notice one kind of hawk, the kestrel, and will shoot any hawk on the supposition that the species is antipathetic to the rearing of game. But now that one was suddenly plunged for the first time into the hawk world, stepping as it were on to another stratum of life or layer in the air, one began noticing hawks wherever one went, so that it was astonishing to see how many there were, previously unsuspected, in just a small circuit of a few miles. It was their wariness which made them escape observation, unless they were being looked for.

I was beginning to be accustomed to the type of cry given by hawks. Gos had several varieties, from his shrieks to his tiny child notes of irritation, whichi-

pipee, eekipip, chip-chip; and each variety of predatory bird, including the little owl, had a special note
which distinguished him from his fellows: yet the
generic type remained constant among all of them, a
beakiness of music which did not come from the throat.
So I noticed that there was something hawkish going
on, the moment I slipped into Three Parks Wood.
Mew cried one voice, and mew answered another.
Then, as it seemed, from all over the wood, the little
voices cried and replied. Cui-cui-cui-cui-cui. It must
have been a family, the parents and two or three
eyases already well grown but not yet driven out. I
was lucky enough to see two of them close. They came,
chasing each other in furious play, darting between
the branches until they were almost upon us: then
they swung round the bole of a tree, showing their
barred underparts in two perfect vertical banks, as if
they were rounding a pylon at Hatfield, and vanished
in the dim leafiness of the full summer wood.

Friday, Saturday, Sunday

They were days of attack and counter-attack, a kind
of sweeping to and fro across disputed battle fields.
Gos had gone back a long way toward wildness with
his first sleep. Each day the ceaseless calls of house-
keeping and lardering called Crusoe away from him,
as his educational needs called him back, and so it
was backward and forward the whole time. Sometimes
he would step to the glove after hesitation, but without

temper, and sometimes he would fly away as if I had come to do him murder. We walked alone for hours every day, Gos sometimes conversing in amicable if puzzled mews, sometimes flapping and bating twice every minute. All the time there was a single commandment to be observed. Patience. There was no other weapon. In the face of all set-backs, of all stupidities, of all failures and scenes and exasperating blows across the face with his wings as he struggled, there was only one thing one could seek to do. Patience ceased to be negative, became a positive action. For it had to be active benevolence. One could torture the bird, merely by giving it a hard and bitter look.

No wonder the old austringers used to love their hawks. The effort which went into them, the worry which they occasioned, the two months of human life devoted to them both waking and dreaming, these things made the hawk, for the man who trained it, a part of himself. I was startled by the upper classes, surprised by the gentleman who allowed a ghillie to gaff his salmon for him — it made the salmon so much the less his — and, with hawking especially, could not understand a nobleman who kept a falconer. What pleasure would he get, taking this strange bird from the fist of a stranger and hurling it into the air? But to the falconer, to the man who for two months had made that bird, almost like a mother nourishing her child inside her, for the sub-consciousness of the man and the bird became really linked by a mind's cord: to the man who had created out of a part of his life,

37

what pleasure to fly, what terror of disaster, what triumph of success!

The end in view was to make Gos come for food. In the end he was to come a distance of at least a hundred yards, the moment he was called, but at present it was enough if he would first not fly away when I approached. Next he had to learn to step to the fist for a reward of food. (The way to every creature's heart was through the belly. This was why women had insisted on the prerogative of being allowed to cook.) Finally he must jump to the fist with one flap of the wings, as a preliminary to increasing the distance.

It was only patience which could achieve this end. I realized that the hawk must be tied to his perch by a leash, and now for three days stood a yard away from him, holding meat out in my hand. I went to him again and again, speaking to him from outside the mews, opening the door slowly, edging forward on feet that moved like the hands of a clock.

Here comes (one thought, suddenly catching oneself out) that excellent piece of work called man, with his capacity for looking before and after, his abilities to reflect upon the enigmas of philosophy, and the minted storehouse of an education that had cost between two and three thousand pounds, walking sideways to a tied bird, with his hand held out in front of him, looking the other way and mewing like a cat.

But it was pure joy, even joy to stand absolutely motionless for fifteen minutes, or while one slowly counted a thousand.

Part of the joy was that now, for the first time in my life, I was absolutely free. Even if I only had a hundred pounds, I had no master, no property, no fetters. I could eat, sleep, rise, stay or go as I liked. I was freer than the Archbishop of Canterbury, who no doubt had his fixed times and seasons. I was as free as a hawk.

Gos had to be taught to know his call. Later on he might get out of sight when being flown at game, and had to be so taught that he could be recalled by the whistle. Most falconers used an ordinary metal whistle, but my escaped soul felt too poetical for that. I felt that Gos was too beautiful to be shrilled at with a policeman's mechanical note. He was to come to a tune, and if I could have played it I would have bought a penny whistle. But I could only whistle with my mouth, and that had to do. Our melody was a hymn, 'The Lord's my Shepherd' — the old metrical Scottish one.

Hawks were taught to come to their whistle by associating it with food, like Pavlov's famous dog. Whenever they were fed the whistle was blown, a kind of dinner gong. So now, as one sidled up to that fierce, suspicious eye, the mews reverberated day in and day out with this sweet highland tune. One came to hate it in the end, but not so much as one would have hated anything else. Besides, I whistled it so sadly that there was always a faint interest in trying to keep to the right notes.

Monday

Gos had on the whole a pessimistic and apprehensive expression, a characteristic of most predatory creatures. We are pugnacious through our inferiority complexes. Even the pike's ironic mouth has a hint of depression in it.

The day was probably typical of training a goshawk, only most austringers had better tempers. It was now nearly a week since I had devoted most of my time and all my thought to him, it was several days since he had begun stepping fairly regularly to the glove, and that morning he had been carried for four hours. So it was not rewarding when the extraordinary creature bated away the moment I entered at two-fifteen. I sat down for ten minutes about a yard from his perch, talking and whistling to him, holding out a piece of liver. He only bated absent-mindedly, so I went to pick him up. Now he bated in earnest, as if he had never seen me before. We had a scene in which at least the master behaved well, and at last we were able to sit down with him on the glove, trying to make him feed. He would not feed. No stroking, offering, nor teasing had any effect. I thought: well, we will go for a walk instead and feed when we get back. The moment the man stood up, with infinite caution and joint by joint, the bird started to behave like a lunatic. And a lunatic he verily was: probably not certifiable, and normally sane enough to outward appearances, yet a sufferer from intermittent delusional insanity. For the next five minutes, inside and outside the mews (the weather had broken again and there was a tempestuous wind blowing, a nuisance which he seemed to attribute to myself) for the next five minutes there was pandemonium. He screamed once, as he had used to do in his first days: it was the scream of a tortured maniac.

Now I too began to lose my temper. The week of ceaseless work, the fears which had always been there lest he should get ill — with the cramp that had killed that boy's eyas spar-hawk, or the keks, or the vertigo, or any other terrible and curiously named ailment which the books spoke about — the culmination also of nervous strain in three nights' watching: it was too much. Probably my unfathomable mind had been initially tending toward ill-humour that day, and this, indeed, may have been the cause of temper in Gos. Hawks were psychic, like red setters, and rage was contagious between unconscious hearts. Anyway, my self-control began to go. I lost it so far as anyone who might remotely dream of calling himself an austringer would dare to lose it: that is to say, ceased to help him back to the glove in the middle of a bate.

When the hawk flies off, in danger of being left to hang upside down, you can induce him back to the glove with a slight flick of the wrist while he is still beating his wings. I did not give this flip. Raging in my heart, I thought: Well then, bate you filthy bugger. Gos climbed back up his jesses, in a worse temper than before; but only to bate again. Now came the sin against the Holy Ghost. After half a dozen more bates

41

an alteration in the portable indoor perch which I had erected so that his sleeping quarters could be

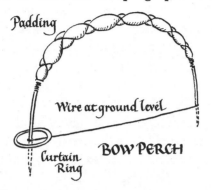

Padding

Wire at ground level

Curtain Ring

BOW PERCH

carried into the kitchen when he was being watched. This perch, which had evolved itself spontaneously, was a perch made out of a tea chest. It looked like this:

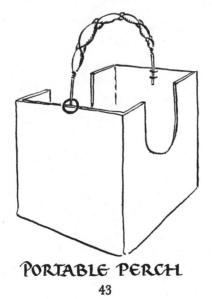

PORTABLE PERCH

Two of the sides of the thing were cut away, so that if he was sitting on the perch his tail feathers could not fall foul of them. The other two sides were too far apart to interfere. There was a heavy stone in the middle to prevent the affair from capsizing when he bated away from it. It was probably an inefficient perch; but it was portable and I had invented it myself. Another merit was that it was highly suitable for people who happened to have tea chests.

By the time the alterations had been completed I had regained the official mastery of my soul, and could think in a direct line once more. I was happy because I had invented a nice perch. I felt that I could face Gos again, and went back to him on the lawn in a good temper, as heaven was my destination. I had recovered my manhood, my equanimous nature, my philanthropic and affable attitude towards the inefficient products of evolution which surrounded me. Gos had not.

He bated when I arrived and while he was being picked up: he bated all the way back to the mews: he bated in the mews, till I popped a bloody kidney into his mouth as he opened it to curse. In twenty minutes, without further transition, he had eaten a whole rabbit's liver and leg, ravenously, as if he had been wanting to eat all the time, together with two or three small pieces of my forefinger and thumb which had been turning the red and greasy shreds for him to get a better purchase on them. Good, I was pleased with this triumph of patience, and erroneously thought that

44

Gos was pleased too. His beak was decorated with small scraps of fur and sinew, and it was my office to clean them off. I lifted my hand to do so, as had been done without protest a score of times since the previous Wednesday. He bated. I tried again, gently. He bated. Again, cautiously. Bate, a worse one. I stood up. He tried to fly to his perch, which was out of range. I raised my hand. He tightened his feathers, stuck out his crop, dilated his eyes, opened his beak, panted a hot and smelly breath, and bated. I got warm and moved too quickly. In a minute it was a dog fight.

This time I was injudicious: but did nothing discreditable to humanity. In the heat and battle of the wings, with which he was striking me on the nose, knocking cigarettes out of my mouth, and for which one was continuously in the terrible fear of broken feathers, I kept repeating a sentence out of one of my books: 'A hawk should never be disturbed after feeding.' But also I was compelled to think that the beak must be cleaned, the authority established, the perseverance not now flouted lest it should be thought of as weak thereafter. I feared to give in lest the hawk should slip back.

After five minutes the beak was clean but Gos was in such a temper that his eyes were starting out of his head. He was a choleric beast. When he was like this it was possible to calm him down by slipping the bare hand over his crop, down his breast and under his stomach. Then, with four fingers between his legs, one

CHAPTER II

Tuesday

WHEN we had dipped the hawk's tail in boiling water and were first able to get a better view of it, a grievous fact had come to light. Gos was suffering from a hunger trace. If a growing eyas was stinted in his food, say for a day or

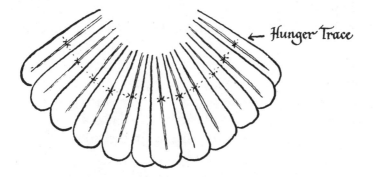

← Hunger Trace

two, the lengthening feathers would add a weak section during those days. The stamina might be picked up again, and the feathers might continue to increase in length, healthy and strong; but always, until the next year's moult, the tell-tale weak section would lie like a semicircular slash across the full grown plume.

It was not that it made any difference from the point of view of appearance, but the feathers were actually weak at the hunger trace, and would probably break off at it one by one. With Gos, two had already gone — one of them before he came to the cottage.

Now a bird with damaged feathers was the same as an aeroplane with damaged fabric: as more and more feathers broke off the bird would become more and more incapable of efficient flight. And, since the feathers rested upon one another, as soon as one was broken the next one to it was liable to go. For this reason broken feathers had to be mended by a process called 'imping'. Most people who have been compelled to read Shakespeare for examinations will be familiar with the word. 'Imp out our imperfections with your thought' or 'imp out our drooping country's broken wing'.

The stub left in the bird was trimmed, a piece of feather corresponding to the part broken off was selected from the store kept handy since last year's moult, an imping needle sharpened at both ends and triangular in section was dipped in seccotine or brine, and the two parts were joined.

Gos had a hunger trace, a visible threat that sooner or later the art of imping would have to be practised on the living bird. The effect of this blemish was to make one frightened of giving him another while his feathers were still growing. (All, except the two deck feathers, were already hard penned.) And the result of this fear was that one's first object was to fill him with food. I did not realize it for many days, but actually he was being fed far too well. The troubles which arose during the previous and the next week were due to the fact that, in ignorance of his normal cubic content, the tetchy princeling had been reduced to a condition of acute liverish repletion. I for my part was trying to teach him to fly a yard or two toward me, by holding out a piece of meat, and he for his part was certain of one thing only — that he detested the very sight of it.

I could think of nothing at first except to continue

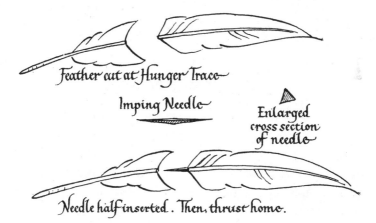

Feather cut at Hunger Trace

Imping Needle

Enlarged cross section of needle

Needle half inserted. Then, thrust home.

the old treatment. I would walk round and round Gos, holding out a rabbit leg, while he bated whenever it came too close: then I would come away without feeding him. There was nothing about it in the books. It became more and more apparent that there was something wrong. His mutes were heavily and with effort dropped, not slashed out with a proud squirt as he had been in the habit of doing, in my eye, and they were bright green. I wondered innocently if he could have eaten some gall with his liver last night? Was his bile induced by his mood or his mood by his bile? The books said nothing about emerald mutes, and so one could do nothing about them. Anyway Gos had not eaten all day, and was in a terrible state of nerves. I proposed to go to bed, to get up at 1 a.m. and to spend the night with him. It gave one the sense of doing something definite at least. 'He shall eat when he jumps to my fist for it, not before,' I wrote hopefully in the day-book. 'Starvation is the only cure for stomach troubles. But perhaps tomorrow give him some egg?'

'He shall eat when he jumps to my fist for it, not before.' If only we had stuck to that sensible pronouncement his training would have been shortened by three weeks. But the mind was a slow adventurer's feeling its way alone in the dark: an amateur's, four hundred years too late for guidance: a tyro's in such curious matters, and terrified by the hunger trace, with the eventual necessity of imping it.

Wednesday

So we were up in the night again, silent among the night courses of the world. Gos was too sleepy, at half past one, to bate away when I went in. I took him out, after he had stepped obediently to the fist, into the bright moonlight where strato-cumulus went fast across a full, pale moon in a north-westerly wind. King Charles' wain was hiding behind a bank of clouds, but Cassiopeia faithfully presided over the north star, and one could faintly see a few pinpricks of the little bear as he hung by his tail. The ghosts of the lonely road to Silston, Adams and Tyrell, were abashed by the moonlight and did not trouble us. Brownie, my red setter, a blue-dark shade, sent Gos into a bate as she scampered through the quiet world in pursuit of rabbits. Evans, in the big house gone to seed, slept in a Welsh peace, dreaming perhaps of Owen Glendower. Chub Wheeler by the Black Pit slumbered deeply, guarded by slumbering dogs. The moon lay calm on the ruffled water. A nocturnal motor bicycle, propably a Silston poacher bent on some lawless errand miles away, just muttered in the silence as the breeze dropped. Standing in the thick grass, with slow heart beats soothed by the still night, I thoughtfully broke wind. The horns of elfland faintly blowing.

When we went indoors again to the aladdin light Gos began to bate. His feet, which had been cold outside, grew hot again, and the hand stroking his soft breast feathers found them damply warm. His mutes still dropped on the tiled floor, green and con-stipated — was it the craye? I sat on the rep sofa, holding him ticking and cheeping on the left hand, while I wrote on my knee with the right. He would beat my head with his wings as he bated. The wrist watch on the right hand ticked. Cheep, tick, and scratch of pen-nib in the crepitating solitude: they slithered like cockroaches over the drum of silence, while down my spinal column the life deeply hummed like a tide. It thundered in far surf on distant breakers, or, like a buried dynamo, droned out its power: used up its steady strength: slowly by wear and tear lowered its efficiency: would eventually run down.

At dawn we went out into the dew, to drink a glass of beer to the sun. The divine majesty, Mithras no longer worshipped, rose with the morning wind, tinting the under sides of dove-grey clouds with other pigeon tints. An owl cried himself away to bed, making Gos look up for a sight of his cousin. The first wood pigeon began his timeless admonition, Take Two Cows Taffy, and a cow heavily breathed.

Now another colour entered the extraordinary pattern. The tense equilibrium and poised mania of delighted solitude would grow thirsty, as it were, after a week or two, for human company: and then nothing would serve but the celebration of drink — not the evening hours with the gentle philosophy of malmsey or madeira, but the gullet-widening carousal of beer among loquacious comradeships, the noise, the rattle, the circular stains, the tock of darts, the smiling faces. For a long time I had not been what one could call an abstemious man.

It was working in my veins now, unsuspected, alongside of Gos. For him, the necessity was a long walk on the fist; as it always was. The chief weapon in training a short-winged hawk was continuous carriage. But for the carrier it became a question of destination; walking all day, one said to oneself:

'Where shall we go now?' Long before six o'clock we had reached the county boundary.

Timmy Stokes, the Buckinghamshire roadman, had cut right up to the end of his beat. The grass stood short and trim, the drains carefully spaded out. Northampton, to be noted with local pride, was neglected and wild. Standing there, in the morning happiness, with a saffron sky in the east and the moon in the south-west still lemon yellow, beside a field where the harvest had already begun, one saw in the mind's eye the imaginary lines all over England: the roads coming up macadamized to the invisible threads, and going on as stone, the ditches suddenly changing from cut to uncut, the parishes and territories and neighbours' landmarks: all slept at peace now, all this beautiful achievement of co-operation and forethought among our fathers who were at peace also, in dust. The meadowsweet in my buttonhole diffused its scent piercingly on the early wind.

As I walked home in the evening it was melted together: the public house five miles away, where I had arrived long before anybody woke up: the hawk chastened and feeding well, even in the bar parlour among curious men: the anxiety and scenes on meeting traffic for the first time; the healthier mutes: the beer slow and swelling in the throat: the warm hearts: the hard body wending its indirect courses: the meadowsweet dead: the red moon perceptibly rising, which I had seen to sink as a yellow one at dawn.

Thursday, Friday

I had cured the bird of his repletion, by means of the fast which he had himself insisted on, and our long watch and longer walking had brought us back to the good terms which existed immediately after the first watch. I now proceeded innocently to stuff him up again, making him eat what would have more than sufficed for a jer-falcon, and at the same time continuing the efforts to make him jump to fist for the food. When he would even step to the glove I fed him, still fearful of the hunger trace.

These two days were characterized by the hunt for food rather than by the carriage of the hawk. Having got it into my head that he was not eating as much as seemed necessary because he was tired of rabbits, I would buy beef steak from the butcher's and spend the generally rainy or windy afternoons trying to shoot him a pigeon.

The day, like all austringer's days, would begin at six o'clock. One would finish writing at about eleven in the evening. Between these times the hawk would be carried for about six hours, and fed three or four times. There was in addition to this the housework and the pleasant occupation of making him spare jesses or other furniture. In the afternoons there was the shooting to be done, and on the Friday I had despaired of a pigeon and shot him a Frenchman — out of season. Gos, while he was being carried, began to keep his eye on external objects rather than on myself,

54

and to bate from them rather than from me. The illegal Frenchman was a great success: half eaten at his evening dinner, with greedy pounces and madly gripping claws.

Saturday

I got up at six o'clock as usual, and for confused reasons decided to get my own breakfast before the hawk's. I was too sleepy to know very clearly what I was doing (one would make plans as one fell asleep and break them when one woke up) but there was some sort of idea at the back of the mind. There were about five great milestones in hawking: the moment when the hawk first ate, the moment when it gave in to its master after the watch, the moment when it flew to his fist, the moment when it flew to him a distance of a hundred yards, and the moment when it made its kill. I have left out the moment when it could be said to be manned to loud noises, bustle and traffic: it was difficult to determine that moment, so the list may be allowed to stand. As the day broke, then, we were still upon the threshold of the third step: we had been trying for days to make him fly for reward, without success. I knew that half the partridge was still left, of which the bird was madly fond, so that greed and hunger might join battle on my side: and I put off his breakfast until after my own, in order that the hunger might be increased.

At half past seven I went out to the mews, spoke a

few words in unlocking the dead keeper's door, confronted the unfathomable raptor. Gos regarded me like the sphinx. I held out the partridge.

It seemed that partridges were not attractive. Rather pathetically trying to cry up my own goods, I turned it this way and that, so that he could get a good view, ruffled the feathers like one of those travelling Indians trying to sell a rug, plucked out a few as if I intended to eat the horrid morsel myself. I could never make up my mind whether I was the master. Gos regarded me with tolerant contempt. He had no doubts about who was the slave, the ridiculous and subservient one who stood and waited. For himself, he had the whole day to fill in.

I looked at my watch and stood still for fifteen minutes, saying: 'I will give him a quarter of an hour.' It meant standing motionless beside the bird, about a yard away from him, leaning forward like a butler and staring out of the door with the butler's distant gaze. Even to look at one's watch, one merely dropped the eyes without raising the wrist. The mangled bird lay in the leather glove, on a plane with the hawk's line of sight, catching the morning sun. The leash was more than a yard long. The hands of the watch went round.

I began to sigh, to straighten myself up, to lower the glove. The time had expired and I began to go away. Began. The reflexes for all these motions were already half way down their nerves, running with the messages of movement to shoulder and knee and back: but before any change had been made, in the moment between the outset and the arrival of the messengers, the great dun-coloured wings had unfurled themselves in half a stroke, the murderous thighs had bent and unleashed themselves for the leap, and Gos was sitting on my shoulder.

An exultation! What a bursting heart of gratitude and triumph (after the first terrified duck) as the ravening monster slowly paced down the arm with gripping steps and pounced upon his breakfast! The rest of the day was a glow of pleasure, a kind of still life in which the sun shone on the flowers with more than natural brilliance, giving them the high lights of porcelain.

Sunday

One had these moments, when everything seemed to conspire to please. On Saturday even the sun came out to grace our feast: and it was a feast, for Mrs. Osborne had asked us to luncheon. Lying on my back under an oak tree in the afternoon, I waited for pigeons as a reward for Gos. But it was such a hot, sunny day, and the chicken and the cream were so comfortable inside, and the light blazed so twinklingly through the leaves, and on my side the shade was so grateful: it became impossible to resent the caution of the pigeons. What a peace-loving but prudent race they were, not predatory and yet not craven. Of all the birds, I thought, they must be the best citizens, the most susceptible to the principles of the League of Nations. They were not hysterical, but able to escape danger. For panic as an urge to safety they substituted foresight, cunning and equanimity. They were admirable parents and affectionate lovers. They were hard to kill. It was as if they possessed the maximum of insight into the basic wickedness of the world, and the maximum of circumspection in opposing their own wisdom to evade it. Grey quakers incessantly caravanning in covered wagons, through deserts of savages and cannibals, they loved one another and wisely fled.

Meanwhile one was still hard at work making Gos with the one hand and unmaking him with the other. No sooner had he flown a yard or two to the glove than he must be given a full crop as a reward. It seemed reasonable to reward his advances. The full-gorged bird would then, of course, refuse to fly at the next visit, because he was not hungry and there was no inducement to do so. Baffled and anxious, one would be driven out into the fields for titbits: a bit of feather instead of fur, some more liver, some tender beef steak, anything to make him come. I ought to have kept him hungry.

Monday

What all this meant to Gos was a thing the educationalist too seldom thought about. For nearly a fortnight now, it must have been a continuous murder in his nervous centres. To me it was a sort of marathon, but one in which I knew the objective and rather less than more how to get there. For him it was all unnatural and all unknown. I sat in a hay-field writing on my knee with one hand: Gos on the other was surrounded by terrible wheeled (like mad eyes) and toothed machines, battered by the thunder of tractors, terrified by strange men. Strange men! I was strange, the machines were strange, the very life and nourishment and sleep in captivity were insanely strange, to the heir of free German eagles who twittered like a skylark on my fist. For two weeks he had been in a nervous pandemonium. Was I introducing him to new things too quickly?

Yet it was sometimes difficult to believe that he was not merely being naughty. Speak harshly to your little boy And beat him when he sneezes: He only does it to annoy Because he knows it teases. Unfortunately the Duchess' remedy was not open to the austringer.

For two weeks he had only fed on the wrist, had been on it for innumerable walks, had come to it quickly enough sometimes of his own accord. But if he was in a bad mood he would still bate from me as if he had never seen me before. Could he be so utterly stupid? He suffered from persecution mania, I thought often, and longed to wring his neck.

Meanwhile the harvest of human people went on. Under adverse conditions and during the worst summer many could remember, the lush grass fell sideways, leaving the whitish under-colour which recalled other and better haytimes. I could not make my friends understand that I was working too. I could not spare the time to help in their emergency, even on one of the two or three fine days spaced months apart. To stop carrying Gos was to let him go back like lightning. All longed to be in the fields, helping in however small a way to get the earth's spontaneous yield safely to store, and one could see the look of disappointment in the farmer's eyes. Any evasion of responsibility to the earth seemed treachery. The hay spoiled, was stacked wet to make sillage: the men cut their hands and went out of action at critical times: but the austringer, sitting dourly on a tree-stump, wrote with one hand while Gos sat on the other and bated at the tractors.

Tuesday

Om, mane, padme, hum. There were fifteen hundred million people in the world, and all of these, of which I was one, would not provide a year's food for one breed of all the fishes in the sea. Of all the quilled creatures which nature in her plethora of species had reared to sing and to prey over the fields of England, and the prairies of America, and the grey, warm tundras and steppes and pampasses and forests and brakes and marshes and jungles and flat deltas and mountain chains and sun-lonely moors, Gos was one, as I was one of the other: so insignificant as to be significant, so transitory as to be eternal, so finite as to be infinite and a part of the Becoming. How should we feel fear or impatience, being so large and small? Rouse, Gos, I besought him, warble and preen yourself: sit, austringer, on God's fist quietly as Gos on yours.

We stood in a field, an object of interest to ten young bullocks who surrounded us. They stood, an interested half-circle or village class, humbly licking the muzzle of the gun (something in the powder must have been tasty, so I took out the cartridges to make it safe) or my pockets, or trousers, or boots. One of them, obviously the backward one, held a straw in his mouth, the personification of rustic ignorance. At last the bold roan, with cool, wet, unslimy muzzle and rasping tongue, licked my left hand: which I, holding out, stood quietly with, as I had once stood in a mountain village in Italy long ago, while the small, humble, grubby children ran to take the stranger's knuckles in their cold fists, for a superstitious kiss.

No doubt the bullocks thought it lucky, like saying good morning to the sweep.

Tuesday, Wednesday
Thursday, Friday, Saturday

One result of this timeless universe, in which sometimes night was day and sometimes there was neither day nor night but only the desire for sleep, was that time itself became illusory. One stood still for fifteen minutes by the watch, but it seemed neither a short time nor a long time: it became merely a time. The concentration on imperceptible improvements became so profound and fascinating that each day became an era, lost all contact with the calendar. Finally, becoming muddled with chronology altogether, I got the idea into my head that the hawk had been in his mews for three weeks when the actual time was really a fortnight.

Thinking that I had been teaching him for three weeks, I began to be frightened that he was not making sufficient improvement: flew into a panic and decided upon drastic forward steps. The puzzles which were always demanding a solution, the way in which one was compelled to invent contingent solutions, the shipwreck which threatened them, and the need to go back to the beginning and start again when things went wrong!

Gos had gone neither forward nor backward, and it seemed more than three weeks. He would step, crooning but suspicious, from perch to meal: but could not be depended upon to jump. One day I managed to shoot a dove for him, and he would eat it ravenously; but my holding the stuff before him, going away if he did not jump to it, merely tended to make him bad mannered. When he did get it he would grab and snatch in a way which was dangerous to me. Something had got to be done.

What I invented to do was this. At night I *loosed*

him in the mews — no leash, and the jesses separate at the ends — and then washed some beef steak in strips.* Next day I intended to give him a strip of this steak at six, if he would come down from the rafters for it, a bit of more nourishing and tasty food (a pigeon's wing) at seven, beef at eight, pigeon's wing at nine, etc. Each time should be a separate visit, and he was to be forced to come down from the rafters if he wanted to be fed at all. It was an admirable plan, and would have worked if I had possessed the experience and courage and patience to carry it out to the end. It was experience that was needed mainly, experience which would make one know that it was really safe to withhold food for several days if necessary, without being visited by that common finale of all keepers of wild animals — finding the canary dead in the cage.

And oh! the agony of patience, the brooding and godlike benevolence which had been exerted. At the thousandth bate in a day, on an arm that ached to the bone with its L-shaped rigidity under the weight of the bird, merely to twitch him gently back to the glove, to speak to him kindly with the little mew which of my conversation he seemed to like best, to smile past him at space, to re-assure with tranquillity, when one yearned to beat him down — with a mad surge of blood to the temples to pound, pash, dismember, wring, wrench, pluck, cast about in all directions,

*A falcon could be got into the desirable state of hungry amenability, and keenness to kill, by giving her a feed or two of beef steak which had been soaked for 24 hours and wrung out. This kept her delicate stomach working, but, the goodness being gone, she remained hungry. It was called washed meat.

batter, bash, tug and stamp on, utterly to punish, and obliterate, have done with and finally finish this dolt, cow, maniac, unteachable, unutterable, unsupportable Gos.

If one could adequately express those early vigils, the uncertainty of their inexperience, the fascination and triumph of their patience: the endless modulations of a voice endlessly reiterating assurance. Mine was a good speaking voice, but no singing voice at all. It had been for weeks a picture of a monomaniac rather tired — one night it would be five hours of sleep, another six — standing motionless on the brick floor of the barn. The floor would be streaked outwards round the perch with white squirts of mutes, so that it looked like a sundial. In one corner there would be a pile of empty jars, in another the disused, rusty oven. All the time there was the housework to do and the food to get. Reflecting upon the latter problems, the maniac would be reciting Shakespeare: *Hamlet*, *Macbeth*, *Richard II*, *Othello*, *The Tempest*, the *Sonnets*. His utterances were supposed to calm and to propitiate the hawk. The man would be the blackamoor now. Soft you, a word or two before you go: he had done the state some service and they knew it. No more of that.

But the tragedy had to be kept out of the voice. Soft you. You were to be quiet, to be patient, to be safe. He was not a blackamoor really, but a rock, a safety, an invariable refuge for winged creatures. They must trust him. Even as Macbeth, even meditating those bloody instructions which, being taught, returned to

64

plague their inventor, the voice was kind and protective. The foulest slaughter provoked the tone only to a world-sadness. Besides, this Duncan — the voice modulated endlessly on, and the hand held out a dead rabbit.

Or it was a tuneless song by candlelight at four in the morning, a voice wandering from tone to tone in the cold barn, while the mind wondered whether the hawk had possibly shown a preference for Gilbert and Sullivan or for Italian opera. On the whole he seemed to like Shakespeare best.

Another picture had been of the man generally not attracted by raw meat, who must stand by the crisscrossed lattice of the window and unflinchingly draw out the entrails of a duck that had just been rather badly shot from behind, with a bare and stinking hand, while the hawk threw pieces of offal and feathers with a head-shake into his face, at which he must not startle the hawk by flinching.

The last picture would show him meeting the postman, a garrulous and charming man with many memories of the late duke. They conversed together for several minutes. The reminiscences about the duke poured on — how he used to take his coat off to help in the saw pit (the headmaster, he noted, who presided over the school which once was the ducal mansion did not do this) or where he had his brickworks. The postman smiled and laughed: so did the austringer, waiting to get away with his letters. But all the time he was startling the postman considerably by mewing at him between his teeth, a reflex action which by now went with patience unconsciously.

'Postscript to tomorrow's plan,' I wrote industriously in the day-book, as soon as I had loosed the hawk in the mews, 'if Gos does not come to me at first I must try staying with him until he does. The idea of staying fifteen minutes in every hour has not worked very well. So I had better finish my breakfast early, take pen, paper and books with me, and devote the day. I can sit on the oven.'

And naturally enough none of it happened. From the first it was unrelieved failure. The deadly bird spent the whole Wednesday in the rafters, refusing to come down. I managed to fight off the fear of his imminent starvation during that day and most of Thursday, attempting every form of blandishment to persuade him into a voluntary approach. I stood for an hour on end, holding out two pigeon's wings with a piece of washed meat between them. I tried silence instead of exhortation, remaining motionless for twenty minutes with eyes half closed. Gos only ruffled up his feathers in perfect peace, stood on one leg and went to sleep. For thirty-six hours now the accursed overlord had eaten nothing, but he would merely sit there ironically and go to sleep. It was too much. On the Thursday morning I suddenly gave him a malevolent glance and left the mews, trembling with indignation. I could have thrown the meat-bag at him.

By the afternoon I had got a step ladder and chased

him from rafter to rafter until a dangling jess was close enough to snatch. I had tied him sulkily to the perch. What I had set out to do had been to starve him into submission, but what I had actually done was to submit for fear of doing so.

Gos now seemed as wild as when he had first been taken out of his basket, and at last I thought that there was nothing to be done except to watch him again for three nights. It was not necessary, but it gave the feeling that something was being done — a needed feeling, when one saw a hawk quite wild again after two weeks' work.

So the second watch began and ended. It was the same as the first. Its details sang in the ear, details of further and further familiarization with an eyas paralysed by fury and overfeeding. I tried to sleep on a camp bed in the mews for an hour every now and then, but it was too painful after a short time: sleeping with one arm held out sideways, supported by a tea case, and the hawk sitting on it. It was a dog's sleep, fitful and shot with starts. The single watcher tended to become bad tempered and to have difficulty in remembering that the almost constant bates were due to fear and not to obstinacy. The hideous, bilious and pot-valiant princeling was upside down as often as he was the right way up, and for the attendant, who must not coerce him by force, patience became almost a physical effort, like running. Patience, hard thing. And sleep: the thought of it was constantly in the mind, with exquisite words of poetry that spoke about it.

From rest and sleep, which but thy pictures be, much comfort. . . .

With breath foul and bulging eye, the panting hawk suffered the first night and much of the next day: the second night was spent in dancing foxtrots to a wireless which stood beside a barrel of beer. It was not that one drank enough to become incapable or stupid, but alcohol now seemed the only way of continuing to live. It was in the second night that one got a kind of second-wind in sleep, an ability to perk up and enjoy oneself, to feel suddenly that it was good and amusing to put a wrist-watch on the right hand with the right hand (the austringer is forced to be uni-dexterous) and to be able to say: well, whatever happens, it has been worth while to be alive.

But at 3 a.m. on the third night I lay down on the camp bed, the hawk having capitulated once more, with Gos on my fist. At four o'clock I rose up purposefully. With eyes fixed in the head, eyes that saw the proximate object only automatically but were strained in spirit on the imaginary goal, the watchman perfunctorily set the hawk upon its perch. He looked not at the bird nor tea chest, but with set, semi-conscious face, a berserk, moved stumblingly to bed. The door was closed, the key turned, by separate and unrecognized fingers. Not Tarquin, not Claudius, more irresistibly pursued their intents. A Frankenstein monster, moving subconsciously, he undressed as he went. Opposition would have been fruitless, bayonets would have been brushed aside, regiments with presented weapons would have opened into a path before those red pupils with their dervish irises which could penetrate man or stone. The boots at the foot of the stairs, the coat at the top of them, the breeches on the floor — in my shirt I tumbled into the double feather bed which had been reserved for guests, but which was now wantonly raped, blue sheets, blue blankets, blue eiderdown, golden bedspread: and there slept unshaken by messenger or trump, until eleven o'clock next morning.

CHAPTER III

SITTING on the floor at ten-twenty in the evening, with a glass of neat whisky and the new wireless set, alone (it was the ultimate bliss to be alone at last) I found a man singing mournfully to some thin stringed instrument. On either side of him the thunderous Sunday orchestras of Europe rolled out their massive melodies: but he, eastern and unbelievable ancient, went on with his unillusioned chant. Where was he, this muezzin, this older civilization? I should not know, nor find him again.

But it was the music of a grown-up race: grown-up, middle-aged, even actually old. Our adolescent exuberance, our credent classical music and full-believing orchestras were pretentious beside his thin recitative. He knew, where we believed. One thought of the march of civilization: the power swinging triumphantly westward with the sun: the new masters springing up in their unnecessary and pubic vigour: Rome and the British Empire. In each case they had fallen back into old age, their horrid vitality evaporated: into being grown-up and no longer needing to assert themselves: into wisdom: into that sad but accepting chant.

How good! To belong to an older civilization: not a dominant one, but one which had reached knowledge. We should reach our own peace eventually. Hitler and Mussolini and Stalin and all the rest of them: they would bring us to the preliminary ruin perhaps in our own lifetime. And then, we should be able to crawl out to knowledge. Out of the waste and murder, out of the ruin, with power eventually gone on westwards, we should emerge to sing uncredulously accompanied by one balalika or zither.

His was a lullaby which knew the fate of man.

To divest oneself of unnecessary possessions, and mainly of other people: that was the business of life.

One had to find out what things were not necessary, what things one really needed. A little music and liquor, still less food, a warm and beautiful but not too big roof of one's own, a channel for one's creative energies and love, the sun and the moon. These were enough, and contact with Gos in his ultimately undefiled separation was better than the endless mean conflict between male and female or the lust for power in adolescent battle which led men into business and Rolls-Royce motor cars and war.

I did not disapprove of war, but feared it much. What did it matter however? It might kill us a score of years before we should in other circumstances die. It was pointless, cruel, wasteful, and to the lonely individual terrible: but it did not matter in the least whether he survived or not. I should be killed, likely, and my civilization perhaps wiped out.

But man would not be wiped out. What did it

matter then? That one dictator for his own mega-
lomania should destroy a culture: it was a drop only
beside the sum of cultures and perhaps a good thing.
In the world which I had run away from I had found
so much wickedness in our present development that
one could have no definite feelings about its termina-
tion: and, as for myself, I was wind in any case.

In the end one did not need European civilization,
did not need power, did not need most of one's fellow
men, who were saturated with both these: finally
would not need oneself.

It did not matter, so long as man survived. If after
the battle this race could be left mature, nothing would
have been lost. Let the Empire and the glory pass
away with a Wagnerian crash, so long as the voice and
the zither still mentioned their patient melody on the
unburdened air. A few peaks of human achievement
would survive: peaks of patience and conquest by
culture: peaks of maturity in education. Since China,
since Assyria, but not since Hitler or Stalin, man had
reconciled the eagle.

Monday

We were back again in the stage of manning the
hawk to the outside world, a stage which entailed
carrying him on the fist all day. It was possible sometimes to relieve the tedium of these day-long vigils by
taking him fishing at Black Pits, where, in the effort
to deceive the subtlety of those large, sly carp which

had probably been introduced there by the monks of Luffield Abbey, it was possible to roll two patiences into one. By tying a string to the first joint of the fishing rod (a string whose other end could be held between the teeth), it was possible to fish one-handed, while the hawk sat on the other, and we did at one time or another kill two fish of about a pound each.

But the amusing thing was that on this Monday, on a spontaneous motion, Gos accepted his first bath. There was a little puddly backwater off the main stew, and in it a heavy board with a nail driven through. I paddled out and tied the leash to the nail, then introduced Gos to the board. He did not want to stand on it at first, for it was low and strange, but soon — ancestrally — he almost twigged. You could see the racial unconscious voice speaking to his bird brain in parables. With an arrogant and dainty motion he stepped on to the board.

I stood back from him two or three yards, with hands on hips, to await developments. When a position was so painful that it had to be changed for another, I moved like the shadow on a sundial. The entertainment was worth it.

Gos cocked his head on one side and stared at the water. Odd, he was saying to himself, probably dangerous, but yet I like it. What is it? He put in his beak, leaning forward with every precaution, to see what it tasted of. (Hawks were one of the few creatures which did not regularly drink water except as a laxative: none needed to be provided for them in the mews.) It did not taste of anything, so he put in his beak again. Curious. He looked over his shoulder at the bigger bit of the stuff behind him, roused his feathers with a rattle, inspected the reeds, the landing stage, me motionless. He thought of flying to the landing stage, less than a yard away, and then gave up the idea. He walked down the slope of the plank into the water. All the time I did not know whether he would accept a bath or not.

Gos stopped in about an eighth of an inch of water and looked at his refracted toes. He bit one of them to see if it was there. When he noticed that it was there he diverted his attention and bit some of the water. He then bit his jesses and the plank, at points where both of them were wet. It was exceedingly strange.

Gos slipped on the wet plank, with an undignified lurch, went into quite half an inch of water, and hurried back to recover his composure. He bit his toe again. It was rather nice.

With the utmost caution he walked down the plank again and considered the possibility of stepping off into two inches. It was evidently a rash step; so he merely made a pass at it with one leg, withdrawing the talon pensively half-way through.

Gos generally looked terrible, terrible in the sense that an eagle or a vulture had that look. In the strong sunlight which shone on the lake — at last the weather was pretending to turn for haymaking — he certainly looked beautiful. But the cruelty had gone out of his

74

aspect. He was only a funny and silly little Gos, whose transparent mind showed him to be an infant still, as it struggled with the elements of hydrostatics.

The sun shone on him, giving him a blue nimbus round his head. The cere flesh about his nostrils was supposedly yellow, as were the irises of his eyes. But that luminous eye (his main feature; it glared out, a focus to all the rest of him, from under frowning brows, the optic of an insane assassin) was genuinely luminous, like the paint on the hands of a wrist watch. Luminous paint, phosphorus: it was blue really, just as much as it was yellow. So the sunlight on Gos took a blue tinge from the hairy whiskers which he wore about his cere and eyelid, carried it on to the eye itself, haloed the whole head in a tint exquisitely elusive, of bird flesh — neither blue nor yellow.

Gos concentrated his attention backward, without looking round, and dipped the tip of his tail in the extraordinary medium. It was fun. He stood and considered the matter, rousing his feathers again. When he roused he looked exactly like a fir-cone. In other manifestations he sometimes would hunch himself up like a penguin, when he was hungry, or go soft like an owl, when he was sleepy.

Now, taking me so much by surprise that I could scarcely keep from laughing, the absurd princeling blew out all his feathers, lifted his tail in the air, and, like an old lady sitting down in a tram or lifting her bustle to get at a purse among the petticoats, sat down suddenly, shiftily, luxuriously, in the puddle. I had

75

never seen a bird sit down before, for the gesture was quite unlike the laying hen's. With ludicrous rapture Gos squatted in the puddle, got up, and, putting his head between his legs, looked at himself from underneath. It was the concentration of attention backward, the strange mixture of pride and affection and anxiety for these parts, the ungainly and somewhat private motion with which he immersed the proud posterior: it was these, and the indignity. The infant Tarquin had suddenly become a charlady at Margate.

Tuesday

It seemed that we were beginning to turn the corner at last. The principle of regulating the hawk's conduct through his belly was becoming clearer every night. I had a plan now by which I kept him in the mews every other day, going to him every forty-five minutes with little pieces of food, but insisting that he must properly jump to the fist in order to get them. I, for my part, would stand before him with the tit-bit, teasing him by voice and gesture, holding the meat just out of reach, giving him an occasional stroke or prod with it, but always drawing back to insist on a real jump. He, for his part, would try every shift to get the morsel without doing his full duty: he would lean forward to the stretch of his balance for a sudden peck, would walk up and down his perch in a torment of indecision, would suddenly strike out a terrible grab with one of his fierce talons, making me fear for my fingers. 'The

Lord's my Shepherd' introduced each visit. Purposely I was beginning to feed him less (although, as the treatment began to be effective, his increasing amenability made one yearn to reward him by feeding him more), in order that he should be hungry enough to jump quickly at the next visit.

I was happy and would sit to read by the fire in the evenings with a contented heart. I found in Barnard's *Mediaeval England* that the Bishop of Ely once excommunicated a thief who stole a hawk from the cloisters of Bermondsey. Some crimes, one reflected, were worthy of excommunication.

Wednesday

On every second day the time-table of visits was varied by carrying the hawk for walks which lasted about six hours, walks which had lost much of their pleasure because the summer had again relapsed into its sullen mood of rain. On this Wednesday, which was windy as well as wet, I shot a high spectacular pigeon, sweeping over in a gust of sousing air. I brought it straight back to Gos, after the rain had wetted me to the skin, and spent the next half hour standing with the hawk in a draughty loose-box trying to make him jump for the leg.

This brought home a new lesson about falconry. The single austringer cannot afford to be ill. Walking home from Tom's in the afternoon there suddenly came what seemed to be a premonition of influenza, the hot, shaking touch of pain and chill. Now what was to be done! With a mind delighted by its interests, a heart soaring to fight such airy problems of bird bones — suddenly the body rose in treachery, raised rebel standards, stabbed one in the back. I made myself hot chocolate, put cherry brandy in it, built a fire in the study and read about Medieval History rather depressedly till bed. If I did get too ill to attend to Gos, I should have to ask the nearest neighbour to feed him twice a day — by putting a brick inside the gauntlet, and tying four strips of beef securely to it, and putting it down beside the bow perch.

Thursday

I got up at six and stood in the middle of the room, wondering whether it was illness. After some minutes, I decided that probably, on the whole, it was not: a decision which was confirmed by experience during the rest of the day.

It was a day typical of this successful week. For fifteen minutes in every hour the man stood before his bird master, holding a pigeon's wing well out of reach, coaxing, whistling, mewing as usual. I teased him by rattling the feathers on the edge of his perch, finally by tickling his beak with them, but always evading the snatch of his clutch. It was at about four o'clock in the afternoon of an otherwise banting day that the monster flew up to my shoulder. I ducked in fear of assassination, and, having recovered courage, got him

78

gently back to glove. He flew thus, an appreciable distance, three times during the rest of the day, went for an hour's walk in the evening, and parted from me at night in an affectionate mood.

My setter bitch, though she scanned my face very closely, could never determine mood from expression. She waited for the tone of voice and, though I tested her with ferocious scowls and beaming smiles, drew no conclusions about the state of mind except by ear, or by recollection of painful or pleasant scenes in similar past circumstances. It was not so with Gos. Not only did he detect my feelings in my face, but by now I was able to detect at least two feelings in his. I could tell by his expression, without the aid of sound or movement, whether he was in a good temper or not. His whole countenance would alter like a human being's. At one time he would be a maniac, his eyes sunken and glaring, his brows frowning, his mouth open, his expression that of a crazy archduke in Bavaria. At the next, beak closed, brows raised, eyes normal, he was nothing more formidable than an infant Gos, ridiculous, inquisitive, confiding, almost a despicable pet.

Friday

In the afternoon Gos went for a walk across the fields to my old friend Chapel Green. A chapel had been built here in the reign of Henry III, and dedicated to St. Thomas the Martyr. When Browne

79

Willis visited Luffield Abbey it was still standing, but had been converted into a dwelling house by splitting it into two semi-detached cottages. The cottages still stood, going rapidly into ruin: and a small farmstead of later date, built just across the way, was following their example. Both were equally decayed. The occasional tramps who had slept in one or the other had left a few comforts — a rotten sack stuffed with straw, or a bit of a box pulled conveniently into a corner. The boys had written obscene remarks in the farmstead — but they had left the ancient chapel undefiled. It stood in the fields, a mile from anywhere.

The place was soundly cursed against man: so it throve with its old virility. Its ash trees were enormous, and its nettles. The setter chased a rabbit out of them, which ran blindly right up to my feet before it turned about and ran the other way. It was a startling piece of life in this unliving place, and it expected to see me no more than I to see it. We took each other for departed spirits, and perhaps the rabbit was one. The parson, I dare say.

The older cottages had been the chapel. In each gable wall the Early English windows and doors remained, filled in with rubble and plaster. It now greeted the visitor fifty yards downwind with a churchyard smell. I looked about me, hardly believing my senses, for it was the veritable smell of death. The ground round the chapel stood higher than the hayfield beside; as all old churchyards did, heaped up with the common and coffinless clay of centuries that had returned to their own dust. I wondered whether there had been a graveyard at the chapel in the old days, and whether, if so, the old bones would be grateful to see a goshawk again. Many must have carried hawks round here ('a sparrow-hawk for a priest', said the *Boke of St. Albans*, 'the musket for a holy-water clerk'), but not for hundreds of years now. The indistinguishable earth felt ready to turn over in its repose, to mutter as farm-labourer's bones muttered when agricultural machinery went by above the tomb, or as huntsman strove to articulate when hounds met beside his grave. The eyes in the earth would have been different to the eyes which confronted one along the roads today; would have looked at the real points, not the imaginary ones; would have been critical and appreciative, immediately noticing the hunger trace and the missing feathers of the tail. The old words still used would have been a link between them and me.

Our forefathers had been small men. Their gloves, their armour, and other few bits, we could no longer put on. The doorway in the chapel gable would have made me stoop.

I thought of the small race now underground, strangers of a vanished species safe from comprehension, almost from imagination: monks, nuns, and the eternal villein. I was as close to them as anybody now, close even to Chaucer 'with grey goshawk in hond'. They would understand my hawk with their eyes, as a farmer understood an elevator. We loved each other.

Meanwhile the smell really was of the grave. A charnel house, some very insanitary and sluttish family of rustic hedgehogs? Gos bated at the smell.

I ran it to earth in a small, square drain, well-head or cellarette (I did not stop to inquire), on the north side of the chapel. It was a dead sheep which somebody had concealed there, rather than take the trouble of burying it. An Amy Robsart of a sheep, shuffled into the same dust as the villein's on holy ground: it was more than dead. Suicides were buried on the north side, I believed. But the deadness of this disgraced sheep was not unpleasant. As I lifted the lid of the drain the flies swarmed out with a roar, leaving behind them millions of those maggots which float-fishermen called gentles. The sheep seethed with them, yellow and pullulating, like a sack of oats poured into the hole: but live oats, busy, dry-sounding, crackling with life. The smell struck against the uvula, giving a dry feeling in the throat. The same maggots had been on the villeins, and would be on me.

I shut the trap door rather hurriedly, but not with revulsion: hurriedly because the smell felt pestilential, although it did not feel unpleasant. I mean that this phosphoric and bony atmosphere had the aura of actually being able to breed disease, which was not in itself an unpleasant thing. It was a thing to shun, but not a thing to regard with loathing. Disease was virile, because it worked. You could feel it with fear, but not with contempt. It was only the things for which I had contempt that made me feel unpleasant.

The air of death, I smelt it vigorously. It was a challenge to life. It was a tonic. The villeins, St. Thomas the Martyr, the Dayrells who had built the chapel, the sheep, and later me: but perfectly acceptable, almost pleasant. They were living and busy maggots, clean, vital, symbolical of an essential life-force perfectly persisting. They were much more lively than the sheep had ever been.

Saturday

The horn woke me, from a dream of foxhunters. The hounds were back in the Ridings again, cub-hunting when much of the hay was still uncarried, and winter had already been prophesied. The men were there in red coats as the sun rose, coats for which they had been grateful at their setting forth: the loud hulloas of encouragement spoke to the young entry amid glimpses of colour and the continual undisciplined noise of guerilla warfare.

As far as Gos was concerned, it was the alternate day on which he was visited at forty-five minute intervals. I was trying to get him to come *at once* to my glove, and now had ceased to stay and tempt him for the full quarter of an hour. If he did not come by the time I had whistled the old hymn twice, I would go away: and it was not until six o'clock in the evening that he was to learn this lesson.

In the intervals of all these visits I assisted at the cub-hunting (it was nice to have the hunt brought right to one's mews) or sat in the sun making spare jesses and leash, watching them. Early in the day there had been two women sitting on shooting sticks, staring blankly at the outside of Sawpit Wood, when a young sow badger came out of it and ran straight at them. An enormous woodlouse made of shaving brushes, a trundling grey hearth rug, the poor, short-sighted thing chose the one part of Sawpit Wood for her exit which was directly faced by those long-suffering women. The women sat with forced and unnatural composure on their shooting sticks, draped about with pet fox terriers on leads, and passed off the badger as decorously as possible. They did not know what to do with it.

The badger solved the problem by trolloping back into the wood, there to be slain some twenty minutes later.

But the sometime fox-hunter had begun to think. They sat there, those two enduring ladies on shooting sticks, and looked at the badger. Women did not naturally enjoy destruction, for their instinct was to create. These two had been made to get up at five o'clock in the morning, when all amounts of paint and powder could make few ladies look their best; had been moved to array themselves in *chic* sporting tweeds and 'sensible' gum boots which yet made it difficult to walk and not comfortably warm in the early hours: had been taken out into an unknown woodland in a heavy dew, with nothing to sit upon but a kind of prop, to participate in a mystery which was beyond

84

their comprehension. Absolutely terrified at heart, they sat there resolutely on the little posts and peered at the wood, convinced that the best method of self-defence was complete inertia. Surrounded by a lot of howling dogs, bustled with apparent aimlessness by two or three howling men in red, they were sure of one thing only: that whatever they did with the badger was sure to be wrong. They looked at it with glassy eyes, and very sensibly did nothing.

It was the enormous hoax of fox-hunting which had brought them out. What a magnificent hoax it was! Lord Hillingdon, who was hunting the dog pack himself, two whips, and the hounds, were having the time of their lives. They were doing something direct: in the case of the peer something very like what would be done when Gos was first flown at a pheasant — if ever I got that far. The master was in the middle of a patient and exciting art, seeking to train his own quadrupeds in the sole and skilful pursuit of another quadruped by direct personal effort. No doubt his eyes were on Rattler or Rantipole with the same anxious apprisal as I could feel in mine on Gos. So far, so true. But at some time in the history of fox-hunting it had been discovered that a Field was a necessary evil. The people helped to hold up the cubs in the autumn, and nowadays their financial contributions often maintained the hunt. A few genuine lovers of the chase (who could be estimated at much less than ten per cent of the average Field) followed Lord Hillingdon because they partly appreciated his about them and so numerous as to make it hopeless to remember them without being sensible: petrified by the suspicion, often a well-founded suspicion, that the horse they were sitting on would fall down and hurt: tangled up in a maze of fears so cunningly contrived that they were finally afraid of being afraid, the unfortunate scapegoats came out twice weekly to their Calvary, and often took to drink in their effort to forget about it in between.

The ostrich when alarmed buried his head in the sand. As far as my two sacrificial victims were concerned, the badger was not there.

But the badger, she too was worth thinking about. She was a young sow, for I opened her mouth and looked at her teeth when she was dead. You could kill a badger by knocking it on the nose, although hounds found it difficult to kill them by breaking them up, on account of the tough skin. The nose was their heel of Achilles. Mine had been killed like that: and now, scarcely torn, was slung over a gate by the whip and left to my reflections, while the riot went elsewhere. Brock: the last of the English bears: I had been proud that her race lived in the same wood with me. She had done nobody any harm. Her home was tidy, her habits industrious by night, her claws and forearms agriculturally strong. Hob would be a good name for a badger.

She dripped blood gently over the gate, while I held up her muzzle in the falconer's glove and looked into her small, opaque, ursine eyes. She was dead.

What could I use her for? Surely, being killed, some definite good would ensue.

But I could think of nothing I could use her for. I could not eat her: I could not make her into shaving brushes or an ornament, because I had a shaving brush and badgers at this time of the year were in a kind of moult: I could not congratulate myself that she was no longer in a position to steal chickens, for probably she never had stolen them. For a little time I thought of skinning and stuffing her head to put beside the fox-mask in my small study, as a memorial to this great day. But I did not want to remember the day. I did not want to remember a young, short-sighted, retiring, industrious, ultimately prolific female who had been turned back by two frightened ladies, cornered by lusty and unlettered puppies, knocked on the nose by a peer.

I was ashamed for poor badger. No skill of mine had gone into her slaughter and there was no sense in it for me. For the hounds there was said to be some kind of sense in this otherwise useless murder, and therefore for the master of those hounds. I was not ashamed for him.

Only, vaguely wishing that foxhounds might confine themselves to destructive animals, I dropped the dead head a little sadly but without recriminations: a 'sentimental slaughterer' as the green-blooded intellectuals put it. Never mind. I was a badger too, in my snug cottage that lay in the badger's wood: and when the war-world came to tear me apart with whoops and halloas, the young sow and myself would be quits.

faster than does the human being — and, in the latter, quick respiration and forcible motion of the heart are a sign of mania. For Gos the world was a place in which life took place on a much more vivid level than on mine, a place in which he could see further and more quickly than I could. For him everything was danger and exaggeration, life was a qui-vive far more taut than anything known to us. However quickly I might have tried to bring my hand toward his head, his head would have more quickly turned in the direction of my hand. Not only could angry words, or frowns, or strangers, or loud noises upset him, but also sudden movements. It had been necessary all through his early manning to regulate one's actions, and as much as possible those of other people, so that he should not be subjected to anything sudden, in sound or sight. This state of affairs, however, could obviously not be allowed to continue throughout his life. For the sake of comfort and peace of mind, it was necessary to accustom him to suddenness, unless I wanted to live the rest of my life in slow motion. Now, therefore, it was necessary to make him tolerate movements less leisurely than what I had been forced to offer him hitherto. Holding him on the left hand, I would raise my right hand quickly to take a cigarette out of my mouth, and the result would be a bate. The movement would have to be repeated again and again, at varying intervals of time, until he was accustomed to quick cigarettes. Sitting on that sabbath kitchen chair, I would suddenly spring up, or move in an unusual way, or speak unexpectedly and loud. Each experiment would have to be repeated a hundred times, until he began to accept me as a spontaneous creature not necessarily static.

Another trouble was that I was dressed in my Sunday suit of black. Until then I had purposely, and perhaps wrongly, worn the same riding breeches and check coat all the time, hoping to get him used to a certain person as seen by his brilliant eye. At tea-time I changed back into the accustomed clothes, except for the stockings. He was friendlier thereafter, although he kept looking at my legs, and it was not until eight o'clock that, having failed to make him come, I took him gently up, gave him a small piece of liver, and carried him without fuss to bed.

CHAPTER IV

DELUDED and imaginative recluse, I was beginning to feel that I could talk about the training of short-winged hawks with experience. It had before been a fumbling among conjectures, with only the printed word to help; but now, inside, there seemed to have begun to grow the personal flower of knowledge. Secretly and not quickly enough to be visible as motion, the roots had begun to push their filigree net through the loam of the unconscious mind. Gently and tenderly the smallest buds of intrinsic certainty had begun to nose out of the stalk, fed with the sap of life rather than theory.

Goshawks were Hamlet, were Ludwig of Bavaria. Frantic heritors of frenetic sires, they were in full health more than half insane. When the red rhenish wine of their blood pulsed at full spate through their arteries, when the airy bird bones were gas-filled with little bubbles of unbiddable warm virility, no merely human being could bend them to his will. They would break before they would bend. 'A fat hawk,' said the old austringer's adage, 'maketh a lean horse, a weary falconer, and an empty purse.' A week of full, bloody crops would send the best reclaimed goshawk in Europe bating from the best hawk-master in the world. Now, at last, I had learned this from the inside of my heart, the first commandment of the austringer's decalogue, a saw of three words which were the beginning and the end of falconry: Regulate the crop. Terrified by the horrible hunger trace which he already possessed, I had spent the weeks of my novitiate in over-feeding him, to guard against a repetition of the ill. No wonder he had refused to come to me, had been intemperate and intransigent, while his small body burned with high living and lack of exercise. He had exercised himself by rage.

I saw now that I must learn to feed him with diligent and minute observation. Suddenly I realized that this was the secret of all training. I had thought before, without understanding the thought, that the way to the heart lay through the belly. The way to government lay through the deprivation of the belly. Every great overlord had known this about my companions in the lower classes. On £90 a year those who lived in workmen's cottages were just on that happy borderland of being sharp-set which kept us out of presumptuous courses. We were in perfectly good health, but not in a surplus state, not riotous, not fierce with surfeit. They kept us efficient and well-manned.

So with good mastery. The trainer of horses had to look first to their oats. I wondered that schoolmasters had not discarded the ferula for washed meat. Perhaps, when I recollected the food at schools, they had: or preferred to run them both together, because of the pleasures of flagellation.

Gos was to be trained now as Napoleon's army had

marched. It was this that must be called the funda-
mental of the trainer's eye in every branch of training
for the blood sports. Those checked and gaitered men
at Newmarket, with their lean faces and bow legs,
ultimately they were assessing the amount of food
given. The lines of the blood horse on which I should
lay my money next point-to-point season would not be
artistic lines, not lines of force or beauty or bone or
muscle: they would be lines of judicious deprivation.
Of course they would not be lines of starvation, but
they would be lines whose axis was the belly. This was
the first law of mastery.

Monday

Gos was hungry enough to make enormous strides,
and at last I was determined to keep him so. It was a
strain and a problem at first, a strain because to reward
him with food was a great pleasure and temptation, a
problem because it had yet to be found out how much
food was necessary to keep him healthy. He had been
fed low for two days now, so that this day I allowed
him a foreleg, a hindleg, two kidneys and half the liver
of a rabbit, feeling that I was being over-generous*
and that he would go back next day. A third of a
pound of raw beef was laid down as the daily ration
for a peregrine, and I reckoned that Gos, being a
tiercel, must be about the size of a female peregrine
and should merit the equivalent of the same weight.

*One hindleg would have been enough.

It was evidently a matter of exquisite assessment which could only be judged by the austringer who knew his hawk (it would vary with different hawks of the same species) — by the austringer whose subconscious mind was in minutely contact with the subconscious mind of the bird. Every alteration in its mental behaviour, every feel of its weight on the wrist, every premonition of greater acuity in the breastbone when stroked: these and all other manifestations must tell the austringer of the fitness of his mate. Too hungry: too flourishing: the exact equipoise was the whole secret of falconry.

The morning was spent in making Gos come quickly to the fist, off the bow perch, a distance up to two yards. He was fed with small scraps at each flight, and he behaved well. In the afternoon he was carried from one o'clock until six, and taken to the main road at Lillingstone Lovell in order to re-introduce him to the motor cars. It was a blazing day (which had its effect in raising his temperature) but on the whole the visit was successful. I sat down with him on tree-stumps, first one hundred yards, then fifty yards, then not more than one yard from the main road: and he bated from nothing except two brightly dressed country lassies who glided by on bicycles. He bated at, not from, a brood of pheasants, and took deep interest in jays and a kestrel which put out of a hedge beside the oats. Home, he came obediently the whole length of a double leash immediately for his evening meal, and ate the rabbit's hind leg in its entirety, finishing bones,

claws and all. It gave him something very like hic-
cups.

Sitting on the night perch of his mews he looked up
at the ceiling, wriggled his head and neck like an eel
or snake dancer from Ind, attempted to thrust down
those three enormous bones into his interior with a
kind of shimmy, regarded me, hiccupping, with glassy
eye.

Reluctant to say good night I stood at the door,
observing this astonishing and vaguely disquieting
spectacle (would he be able to digest such a mouthful?)
and thought about the morrow. It had been a splendid
day. He would go back. He was sure to. Goshawks,
and this was the second thing I had learned from
experience, went back two paces every time they went
forward one. 'There is no short cut,' said the good
book, 'to the training of a Gos.'

Tuesday

I supposed that what I was going to write eventually
would be the kind of book which would madden every
accomplished falconer, and I was sorry that it should
be so. I could imagine an aged austringer sitting at
the very top of the tree which I was now so laboriously
climbing. He had a pettish and know-all expression,
soured by years of contact with intractable goshawks.
So much of his patience had been absorbed by these
creatures that he had none left for his fellow mortals.
In appearance slightly crochetty — he would be wear-

ing a twa-snooted-bonnet, and his long white mous-
tachios would be waxed at the ends — he sat at the
top of the ladder and proclaimed that he had been
manning hawks for sixty years. What right had a
cowardly recluse who fled from his fellow men, said
he, to write about these almost fabulous creatures?
Fools, he remarked in a very pouncy way, rushed in
where angels feared to tread.

But I was sure of one thing that I still loved, and
that was learning. I had learned always, insatiably,
looking for something which I wanted to know. Of
all things which I had begun to learn or thrown aside
almost at once, the most wildly yet tranquilly and
enduringly happy had been the mystery of the divine
salmon and his exquisite fly. Perhaps, in the end,
giving up all other attempts, I should grow middle-
aged and acquiesce in my second-hand destiny,
which would be to lie beside a highland ripple in
which my monster dwelled. Meanwhile the search
continued, and with it the necessity of earning a living.
It was easier to combine the two: to learn and then
to write about it, thus making money out of what one
loved. I determined to tell my aged austringer to
come down out of his tree (an American idiom)
because mine was not a falconer's book at all. It
would be a learner's book only: in the last resort, a
writer's book, by one who might have tried in vain to
be a falconer.

I was proud of Gos. He flew to the fist quickly,

though not far, for a small tit-bit, when taken up in the morning. He ate, coming a yard or two, much of the flesh off a large rabbit's leg, given in small repeated offerings before noon. He was carried without unusual scenes from one o'clock till six, except for a small interval when I had to go off and shoot a rabbit, and then I decided to try him on the creance.

A creance is a long length of twine, strong string or fishing line, not too heavy for the hawk to carry in flight. Usually, I believed, some assistant would carry the hawk while the master called it, tied by the creance, from the assistant's fist to his own. But I had no assistant, and preferred not to have one.

I set Gos down on a quiet railing and tied the creance to his leash. As a fisherman I was fond of knots, could indeed occasionally entertain myself by tying the blood knot, which Chaytor made romantic and famous as well as beautiful (which it had been all along), on odd bits of string. But now the knot had become a thing to fear as well as to love. At the other end of it there was a bird momently more valuable than anything one had ever possessed, and one of the few things left that one did possess. Ceaselessly, day and night, the neat and ingenious knots of his jesses, the falconer's knot by which his leash was attached to the ring on the perch, the slip of the jesses on to the swivel, and of the leash through the swivel, these became critical and not untouched with fear. The suspicion with which the salmon fisherman makes all sure became a part of falconry, and one never tied a knot without the anxiety of a turnkey and a faint dubiety at heart.

My creance, which was made of brand-new tarred twine, was twenty-four yards long. At the end remote from the hawk — that is the end which was tied to the railing — there were bound in two yards of strong catapult elastic so that he should have no chance of snapping it by a sudden jerk. I stood twenty yards away from him — with the result that he would in any case have a surplus of four yards slack — and began to whistle the accursed hymn. He had previously shown himself much fascinated by the rabbit.

I must have gone on at this for an hour, sometimes giving up for a moment and lying down among the cows (who had just come out from being milked and caused some anxiety by sauntering over the creance, as it lay stretched in a double line from the railing outwards for ten yards and back to the hawk), sometimes standing up to redouble my efforts. The problem was to make Gos understand that though he was still tied he was now free to come those extra nineteen yards.

I tried coming nearer, up to six yards, but he was still bemused. Taunted by the feeding hymn, whistled from a distance which he had never before been free to fly, the unfortunate tyrant blew out his feathers to their full extent, paced up and down his railing, glared about in all directions and practically bit his finger nails with indecision. I tried tweaking at the length of the creance between him and me, holding the twine in the hand which flourished the rabbit as a lure and jerking it in time to the 'Lord's my Shepherd'.

After more than an hour of failure I decided upon what I took to be drastic measures. Standing ten yards away, I pulled Gos off his railing by means of the creance. He fluttered to the ground and flew back. After more tweaking I pulled him off again. Again the same, and again and again.

At the fourth attempt he remained on the ground. Picking his way between thistles he hopped to and fro, finally in my direction. I retreated before him as you do when training a retriever. Skipping and leaping, fluffed full, a terrible toad, he bounded in my train. The last two yards of the twenty-four were flown to the fist: and the reward was, before he went to bed, a good two-thirds of a crop of fresh young rabbit.

Wednesday

At this time two interests were going on simultaneously. There was the excitement of hoping to accomplish the fourth or penultimate great step of his education — the moment at which I wanted to see him fly one hundred yards on his creance — and there was the bother of getting him properly manned to the surrounding world. Living as we did in a wood, so far even from a road, his had been a sequestered life with few novelties. Seeing so few strangers, meeting no motors unless carried a couple of miles to do so, he was at present unaccustomed by habitat as well as by instinct to the bustle of the modern world. Yet he had to learn to stand that bustle, as we all have to do, however little we visit it.

On that Wednesday, determining for the first time to hazard him against the gentle traffic of a country town, I walked to Buckingham and back, in order to introduce him slowly. He stood it well, except for two bad bates, one on entering the market square and one on leaving. His bates at the people were less annoying than the people's reaction to him. Nervous mothers wheeled their children's perambulators to the opposite pavements, exclaiming women stepped out on the road in front of motors, rather than pass us within a yard, while troops of children followed us about. To evade this nuisance he was left in a back room of the Swan and Castle for half an hour, while I did my shopping.

It was a great joy to shop in Buckingham, especially when you had a shopping list which began with 'bit of ribbon for kitchen curtain' and went on through 'leather for lure, two big staples and bit of strawberry netting, scales, stronger string, rabbit nets, blue paint for door, screws and nails, seccotine, good penknife, darning wool, cotton, needles', until it reached 'Bert's *Treatise of Hawks and Hawking*, For the First Time Reprinted from the Original of 1619, with an Introduction by J. E. Harting, Librarian to the Linnaean Society of London'. For you were more likely to come across a copy of Bert, of which there are only about 102 in existence, in the ironmonger's or the saddler's at Buckingham than you were to find it at Bumpus or the Bodleian. There was a kind of glory about the backward parts of the better shops in Buckingham, in which you might find anything. If I had wanted a battle axe, or a quiver with some arrows, or a pair of skis, I should have found at least two of them at Herring's: while I was sure that Mr. Evenson could have found for me, somewhere about the premises (if only he could put his hand upon it), an eighteenth-century coach or a billiard table.

Sated with these excitements, and with the walk of twelve miles, we got home at eight o'clock. The hawk did not like cars or cyclists or numbers of people, but if he were in a good temper he could be persuaded not to bate from them. It was perhaps in this side of manning that he was most backward of all, and I could not really assert that he was at ease with my own right hand. All the way home I had been boresomely jerking it about at varying intervals to accustom him to its movements.

We got home at eight and he was put at once on the creance. Immediately, or at any rate after less than five minutes of hymnody and hesitation, the great bird was sailing owl-like through the twilight. I cowered as my master stooped upon my shrinking shoulder, and then gave him gleefully five ounces of beef steak — previously weighed out on the scales — deciding that on the morrow the ration should be increased to seven.

Thursday

I lay in the long grass at Silston cross roads with Gos on the fist. The cars came past pretty regularly there. It was shady where we lay, with a good breeze keeping the trees alive, two men making hay in the fields opposite. Gos himself stood with full fluffed feathers and semi-contented eye, meditating standing on one leg. When he was in a good humour he would rouse his feathers, and this would leave them ruffled. Before he had done this, while the feathers lay close and sleek, you might be sure that he was not content. But if he had done it, and if he began further to stand on one leg, then you knew that you were in for peace.

It was a lovely day, and Gos was being as good as gold. He stood there, lifting the spare leg with clenched talons in tentative thrusts: a monocular or uhlan-officer expression on his face, as the eye remoter from the sun dilated more than the nearer one.

It was a scene perfectly idyllic — until another of the cars came by. Then down would go the rising claw, the erect posture would be lost, the hawk would flinch upon the fist with mad round-questing eye that meditated a bate, the feathers lying flat to his body.

I lay in the warm afternoon and thought about Gos. If one were to give him a proper name, what should it be? Hamlet would be suitable, or Macbeth (as he was subject to illusions): then there was Strindberg, or Van Gogh, or Astur, like the giant warrior in Macaulay (the hawk's Latin name was Astur Palombarius): there was Baal, as in the poem by Kipling, or Tom (he who had the host of furious fancies), or Medici or Roderick Dhu ('fierce lightning flashed from Roderick's eye'), or Lord George Gordon of the lunatic riots, or Byron, or Odin, or Death, or Edgar Allen Poe, or Caligula, or Tarquin, or, for his happier moments, Gos: a cross between a gosling and a goose. Reflecting upon this problem I decided that the best solution would be to call him all of these. The last Duke of Buckingham had been called Richard Plantagenet Temple Nugent Brydges Chandos Grenville, and I could derive my goshawk's lineage no lower than his.

On the way home Gos had a proper bath in a roadside ditch, ducked his head, toppled over, flapped his wings, splashed, paused to meditate and scratch his chin in the middle of it: all in the lovely sun and ripple.

At six o'clock we went out to the well and he was set down on the railing which enclosed it. While at Silston, half a pound of beef steak had been bought, and this had been divided into two equal parts. (The hawk had been given a rabbit's hind leg that morning.) I had been out previously to the well and measured a piece of twine fifty yards long. One end of this was attached to the rail of the well, the other end extended down the ridings to its full extent. It had been doubled then back to the place where it was attached, so that at the well head there were two ends of twine, one tied and the other free, while a double string stretched twenty-five yards to its bend which lay in the grass.

I put Gos on the railing and retreated to a distance of forty yards, giving ten yards law in order to prevent his being checked in flight, and began to call and whistle. The pursed lips repeatedly proclaimed the Lord their Shepherd, urgently, caressingly, madly, nobly, slowly, rapidly, continuously, with pauses. 'Dinner!' they blew, commandingly, pleadingly, majestically, rapaciously. 'Come along, Gos,' they panderingly, whiningly, peremptorily, softly articulated. 'Now, now,' they remonstrated, feeling rather thankful that this could be done without an audience, 'don't be silly, come-along, be-a-good-Gos, Gossy-gossy-gos.' And Tiddly-tum, tiddly-tum, Tiddly Tum Tum repeated echo to whistle, whistle to echo.

For nearly ten minutes the extraordinary uproar went on in the still ridings. So far away that even his flaming eye could no longer be distinguished, the loved goshawk stood with his back to me, turning his head this way and that. At last he turned upon the perch, roused his feathers into a greedy puff, began to hop upon the railing. The pleas, the tuneless whistling, the staccato notes rose to an orgasm of lust for beef: in vain. They relapsed into the majestic, the quiet, the filled-with-silence pauses. Suddenly, after ten minutes during which he had cocked his head at the creance and visibly pondered its reliability as he moved about, suddenly, and without relation to the pathos of my music, sweet Gos began to fly.

To fly: the horrible aerial toad, the silent-feathered owl, the hump-backed aviating Richard III, he made toward me close to the ground. His wings beat with a measured purpose, the two eyes of his low-held head fixed me with a ghoulish concentration: but like head-lamps, like the forward-fixed eyes of a rower through the air who knew his quay. The French called him *rameur* as well as *cuisinier*. Too frighteningly for words (when I had taken him up to bring him to the well — and given him the shred of beef with which he was always rewarded for a voluntary jump — he had flown to my shoulder and fixed his talons in the un-protected flesh, taking me by the scruff of the neck), too menacingly he flew, not toward the at-right-angles-held-out beef, but directly toward my face. At five paces nerve broke. I ducked, still holding the beef at the stretch of my arm, and stayed cower-ingly for two beats of the heart.

But the sudden movement, or the sudden discovery of the red setter fooling about in the long grass at my side, had put him off. Before I could see where he had gone, while I was still bunching together for the strike, Gos slewed off on a miss-stoop, flew to the nearest tree of the riding, missed his grip of it because the creance caught him short (very luckily), hung inverted for a moment, dropped into the hedge.

I called him for another few seconds, and then, going to disentangle him, took him back to the well-head. For letting me pick him up without protest (he jumped to the fist) he was rewarded with another shred of beef.

We started again. This time, after only five minutes, the attack was launched again. I stood to my guns. Imminently confronted with death, stared in the face by those two Athene-noctua eyes which were coming at my head rather than at the beef a full arm's length away from it, I braced the breast muscles not to flinch. It was too much. At two yards humanity became again the inherent coward, and cringed away to the right, averting face from the eyes of slaughter, humping shoulder, powerless to remain erect. But Gos bound to the shoulder with a decisive blow, stepped quickly down the arm, was feeding on two ounces of beef.

When he had eaten it (and tried to eat the paper — which had been kept as a visible lure) I took him back to the rail. He left me for the rail reluctantly and avariciously, insisting upon taking the paper with him. After I had returned to the distance of forty yards, which had increased by five, he dropped the paper and, showing more interest in it than in me, jumped down to make a final test of its edibility. I waited till he had jumped back to the rail.

Now, for the third time, the calls were reiterated: and then, with less than a minute's pause, the brooding death was launched at the face. I stood, and scarcely more than an inch or two flinched: for the second two ounces of beef steak Gos came quickly on a creance nearly fifty yards.

Friday

There was no progress at all that day, and not to go continuously forward was to go back. How often, and for how long periods, did human life suddenly dumb-strike and confuse itself: becoming as it were curdled or criss-crossed, the surface not coherent and the grain influent. This solitary life was one of almost boundless misdirected energy, but even misdirection was a form of direction. For months at a time I was content with that. Then suddenly the blow fell, a kind of stroke like that which afflicted Orlando, and even misdirection failed. All kinds of going and doing turned inward upon themselves, incestuous cannibals, and like the serpents of Limbo consumed their tails. Nothing served, nothing wanted itself to be done, nothing went forward.

Sullenly and shiftily I lay abed until nine o'clock, fetched Gos to his bow perch after an abortive effort to make him feed on a creance, watched my chimneys being swept, hemmed curtains, made a stiff catapult, tied up a new full-length creance with its two yards of elastic at the hook end, arranged tools in a tool-box in the coal shed: but all the time knowing that I ought to be walking to Silston with Gos, in order to man him to the road traffic and village life: all the time not wanting to do any of the things I did, and doing them ill. It would have been better to have lain insensible.

What was it that man wanted and what force made him always so bitterly to strive for it? At last we should come to nothing, with all our creances in a tangle about us, our curtains unhemmed and unravelling, and the tools confused and broken.

Saturday

Festina lente, as one did when pouring out a bottle of Guinness. The devils had vanished next day as suddenly as they had appeared, and the weather seemed really to have set in for good at last. A late summer or blazing autumn, the world had turned to fire just as the barley came down and after the oats. The motionless air was everywhere humming with the tractors and elevators as the last hay went to the rick. The tines of the elevator marched incessantly upward, a metal cavalry like the jingling squadrons of the harrow, but more sedate. In a double and inexorable rank their endless mobilization stormed the hayricks, an army with banners.

In the ridings the free beasts lay motionless under the tree-shade, horses under one tree, ewes under another, bullocks under a third. Only their tails flicked. The austringer, with two miles to cover across country to the nearest main road and compelled to wear a coat in order to save his arm and shoulder when the hawk dropped on them off the creance, paused in the hedge-shade after each gate, getting his breath again as it were for the almost physical immersion into sunlight as he crossed the next field. It was a series of dashes across the desert, a series of endurances which were summed up field by field in advance, a series of dives into the scorching air which partook of a blue sky almost violet with heat.

The farmers and their men had in one day gone a deep mahogany: their faces had resolved themselves into the lean lines of the brown skull, gaining much in power and character and passion. The eyes were deep in tangled crow's-feet. They and the white teeth gleamed more in contrast with the flesh, so that everybody gave a vivid impression of humour and madness. It was the harvest mania.

Nothing in forenoon, noon, or afternoon moved in the ridings: only the wise and timid pigeons, so clever at coming out on the opposite side of a tree and instantly swooping downward for the cover of the hedge in which it grew, made a fore-running in front of the austringer, leaving the green seclusion in which they had been 'listening the pleasant sutherings of the shade' with a loud clap of their wings.

The hawk bated toward the shade of each tree as they passed it, sitting in the intervals with open mouth and protruding tongue. The arm, which would carry the bird in rigid right-angularity from ten in the morning until eight o'clock at night, with only an hour's break for what masters called luncheon and men called dinner, began to ache increasingly as the burning sun descended. Late and languid, with the hawk fed and mewed and the bitch baited, the austringer made a luxurious meal of cold salmon, while the full harvest moon burned outside. She was no longer an exhausted and reflecting satellite, but a living personality; she also was afire once more, a shadow-caster brighter than the headlights of a car.

All day the heat raised Gos's temperature and made nothing suit. He bated at almost every car on the Silston turning, and refused to come on his new creance at Tommy Osborne's. I had tried to feed him there at seven o'clock, not wanting him to associate a particular place with coming to the whistle. But there was too much doing. Baulked by inquisitive bullocks, distracted by the comings and goings of the farm, myself faint from heat and hunger while he from both was far from temperate, we had to give in. I wound up the creance and plodded back to the cottage, tied him to the well-head, paced off seventy-five yards, and began to whistle. It was a day of almost unrelieved failure, one of those days in which one worked long and hard without measurable reward except the knowledge that one had worked. I held out the lure with an arm almost palsied and a heart quite unexpecting. After half an hour I would give in, take him up, and feed him without a conquest.

But before The Lord had been my Shepherd for one bar, he was coming. Surely, low to the ground, well-mannered and without panic, he was beating all that long distance with his eyes fixed on the food. The creance made a little whisp of disturbance in the long grass as he carried it after him. He ate two ounces. I hurried back to the well-head, deposited him, ran back a hundred yards with my heart in my mouth lest he should follow before I was ready — he meanwhile crouching on the bar full-fluffed and ravenous — and began to whistle again. It needed two verses of the signal-hymn, during which he hopped on the bar of the well-head — and here there flashed through the mind all those things which have not been described in my book, the dangers of the creance catching short on snag or thistle, the necessity of keeping all clear, the mental alertness which was needed to keep all details (and how much could go wrong with how little in this world) clear in one's head, and the quickness of the decision in acting in one way or another in the face of emergency, training desiderata and accident non-desiderata being summed simultaneously and instantaneously — but while they flashed the gos was coming again. It was not that he came. At a hundred yards, the first time he had ever come this distance, it was a question of 'was coming'. It was a matter appreciable in time.

Thus, when being seemed hopeless and nothing left but to endure, often God would turn a kind face in real reward for labour and, at a dark moment, surprise with his present: so much more lovely as a surprise.

I did an unwise thing, but could not help it: gave Gos a full crop of beef (four ounces) new-bought at Silston, a sparrow, and the foreleg of a rabbit. Stuffed full, startled by the unusual generosity, on the point of making a Falstaffian belch, Gos said good night in the burning moonlight with a rather dazed expression: and I, writing up the day-book in the circle of the lamp, cried Prosit loudly and repeatedly, quaffed fiery liquids of triumph, drank damnation to all enemies, and smashed the glasses on the floor.

CHAPTER V

WELL, there it was. The job was practically finished and it had turned out not to be such a difficult one after all. In a few days I should catch two or three wild rabbits alive in my nets, and, when Gos had killed these on a string in the open, which was illegal, he would be ready to fly loose. I could flatter myself that he was practically made, although his manning to crowds and motors was still behindhand. I breathed the air of achievement with some displeasure. It was easy. I should have to find something more powerful to pit myself against next.

It was this that had been working in my mind for several days now, since I had bought the big staples and the strawberry netting in Buckingham. It had been there unconsciously since I first saw the supposed sparrow-hawks in Three Parks Wood, so many weeks ago. Now the boy, who had helped me to dip that distant tail in boiling water at the beginning, was writing to say that a sparrow-hawk which I had kept for him, had been allowed to escape, and that he was without a hawk. I wrote back that I knew of a pair and would try to catch one for him.

Almost certainly vain promise, these were 'haggard' hawks, the adult creature in the wild state: and I was not even certain of their species. I had only seen them once or twice, and circling so high up, and with such little knowledge in myself of hawks. I had been accustomed to think of only the kestrel as 'a hawk' and to shoot at him when I could. So far as I knew, the kestrel hunted the fields by preference, had a long tail like a cuckoo, and hovered motionless in the air by inclining his angle of incidence against the wind or possibly by finding thermal currents of upward air. He agitated his wings occasionally by a rapid fraction, had a red back if you had a chance of looking down on him, with whitish underparts, and was a slim, long-bodied, long-winged-looking bird. He was the common churl, the medieval villein.

The hawks in Three Parks Wood did not hover: they circled in the way which falconers aimed at when they taught the reclaimed peregrine to 'wait on': that is to say, they sailed round and round at a good height. Their tails seemed short in relation to their breadth of wing, and they were compact in appearance. They seemed to spread their tails in flight, where the kestrel usually held his shut like a fan. They hunted the wood rather than the fields, and were generally to be heard in it. They were a pair, with perhaps a family unless they had by now driven the youngsters out: whereas the kestrel seemed usually to be a bachelor peasant. They were in the wood much more often than not, mewing to each other as they hunted in couples. I had only seen them close once, as they chased each other in play a month before, and then I had not known enough to notice whether their wings were rounded or pointed. They had struck me, in the fraction of a second as they sped round the tree, as having the speckled or *barred* or at any rate mottled khaki underparts which I remembered in the boy's sparrow-hawk.

I was pretty sure that they were not kestrels, though not sure; could not dare to hope that they would be the cliff-haunting peregrines of Scotland and Wales: and so I called them sparrow-hawks.

Sunday

The new craze was in full swing, and I spent nearly all the day making a bow net. It cost the price of two yards of strawberry netting, four large staples and hours of experiment.

The pegs were of hazel, the bow of ash freshly cut. The bow was hinged to its staples by leather joints. When set, it lay in a semicircle on its pegs: when sprung it pulled into the complete circle of shaped netting, which took two hours to knot into shape. On the diameter of the bow there was pegged down a stout section of rough branch with a metal loop in the middle of it. The theory was that a lure — a live pigeon or blackbird — should be tethered to the loop on the rough branch: that the spar-hawk, observing this morsel from above, would stoop upon the lure; and that the austringer, nasconded some fifteen yards away, would pull the string, thus enclosing both lure and spar-hawk in the meshes of the full circle. On the

116

whole, the principle was similar to that of the old-fashioned sieve under which small boys used to catch hungry birds in winter.

When all this was completed, and the leather found to be working firm and easy, I walked over to Tom's cottages and enlisted the aid of Cis. Tom had said that I could borrow four hurdles, and these Cis carried up

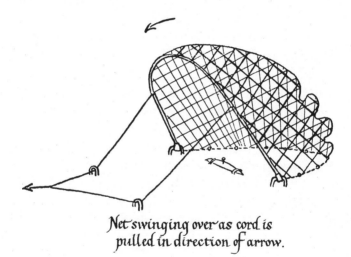

Net swinging over as cord is pulled in direction of arrow.

to the wood: while I trudged beside him, carrying the bow net, the creance, the falconer's bag, a bill-hook, and Gos.

We set to work. In an hour's time there was a hide in the wood, thatched over the top and up the sides with green branches. Fifteen yards away from it the bow-net lay in its open semi-circle, strewed with moss, and leaves, and small twigs, and dust rubbed between the hands.

While these things were going forward it had been necessary to see that Gos was not neglected. Any cessation in attention to him resulted in a return to savagery, and so one had to try and keep his education going at the same time. My method of transport about the countryside was the bicycle, and it would be convenient if I could teach him to come with me on the handle-bar. So he spent the morning sitting on a new perch tied across the bar — but had an accident with it when left alone, by bating at some small intruder and pulling the bicycle over. (I reflected, as I picked him up, that after a course of falconry any man would make a good mother.) Then he was carried round the ridings for half an hour, while the bicycle was wheeled with the other hand, and now, after the hide had been finished, he was made to come a distance of fifty yards on his creance, twice, in a strange milieu (no longer from the well-head, that is to say, but away from home) and in the presence of a stranger, Cis.

Walking home tired in the Sunday dusk, it became obvious that it had been a good day. While one was in the act of being busy with these small creations, the mind travelled lucidly about its humble errands, gently skirting and mantling round the little problems of ash or hazel. Pre-occupied with simple, tangible constructions, looking before and after, the Biscay of the brain was stilled to a sweet calm: and in this calm vague thoughts created themselves unconsciously — sudden, unrelated discoveries. My fingers had stopped in the middle of a knot in the bow-net, struck by an unsuspected ambiguity in the answer of the Pretty Maid. Having all through childhood a well-founded suspicion that my parents would only tell me of anything spicy with the best intentions, I had assumed that the milkmaid, in answering the gentleman who could not marry her because her face was her fortune, that Nobody Had Asked Him, was delivering a nasty snub. Suddenly I doubted this.

> Then I can't marry you, my pretty maid.
> Nobody asked you, sir, she said.

Nobody asked you to *marry* me.

As I put Gos to bed in the darkness, a new thought emerged. This time it was a quotation: To scorn delights and live laborious days. But it presented itself the other way about, saying: To live laborious days for their delight.

Monday

The next thing was to catch a blackbird; a feat reasonably easy in the winter time, when hedges were bare and hunger made them tamely come for crumbs, but not so easy in the profusion and wildness of late summer. I could think of no sure means except bird lime, which was illegal. For that matter, nearly everything concerned with falconry was illegal: our modern legislators, busily passing laws for urban criminals, had forgotten altogether, or never heard, that hawk-mastery existed. Half the things we did were forbidden by laws recently passed to curtail quite different activities: the other half were presumably still governed by laws passed before Elizabeth, which nobody had troubled to repeal. I believed, for instance, that under one of the latter kinds of law I was legally able to go hawking on all my neighbour's property without asking his permission, while under one of the former I was hardly allowed to hawk at all. In this state of confusion I thought it better to remain unacquainted with any law, while attempting to be as humane as possible.

I took Gos to Silston, the great poaching village of the neighbourhood, and hence the village which knew most about birds and beasts, and there we made inquiries about bird lime. The second person I asked, merely an unknown pedestrian who had passed the time of day and fallen into conversation about the beauties of Gos, was kind enough to bicycle a mile after me, bringing the advertisement of a firm which supplied this commodity. It was illegal, it seemed, to use bird lime, but not illegal to advertise or sell it. However, I was now set upon other courses.

There was a packet of size in my coal-shed, size which I had used for the walls upstairs. You mixed. . . .

But why define these endless mixings? Heavy machine oil, size, paraffin, water: on a stove in the garden I brewed these liquids and any others I could lay hands upon. Everything dried to the consistency of marble, and to this consistency it dried in less than two minutes. The shades varied from jet black to toffee, a challenge to Michelangelo but not to the birds. At three o'clock in the afternoon, turning with a sinking heart from these loathly preparations, I found a wandering publican of my acquaintance leaning over the garden gate. It seemed a direct providence, for he had a car, and before anybody could say knife we were in Buckingham: where, within a few minutes I had bought a new wireless set, two tame pigeons in lieu of blackbirds, and all the bird lime I wanted. I procured the lime quite easily by stopping X, who was passing in another car, and reflected that it was very lucky that I had once stood X a drink in the Swan and Castle. So much for law and order.

The day degenerated into beer, argument, darts and skittles, at public houses over half the countryside. Afterwards we came home and had an argument until half after midnight. Since (I realized next morning), the publican had been arguing about the Grafton hounds while I had been arguing about the licensing laws, no definite conclusion was then reached.

In the course of this intemperate and wasted day, Gos had been taught at odd moments to tolerate being carried at low speeds on a bicycle, and I had done my best to man him to motor cars by getting the publican to drive along beside us in bottom gear, talking to us through the window. But I was relaxing my pressure

the well, about a hundred yards away. I had walked quite half this distance before I realized that Gos was no longer on his rail.

The setting in motion of the car, and the sight of his master running in front of it, must have upset him. He had flown to the full length of his creance, and was now sitting in the outermost twigs of a high oak which had no branches for the first ten feet. He had managed to spin the creance in and out of the twigs, and was sitting composedly in a kind of cocoon.

I informed him that the Lord was my Shepherd, waving beef and a handkerchief. I stupidly tried to pull the creance from the well end. I ought to have loosed the well end, annoyed him so that he bated from the tree without impediment from behind, and taken him up when he came to the ground. However, I did the other thing, which came more naturally, and this caused a bate, and the cocoon became inextricable. A fact which made matters much worse was that the creance itself, of tarred twine, had turned out to be of poor quality with hardly any breaking strain. It had already been broken twice in spite of the elastic.

I fetched a ladder and solicited the aid of my nearest neighbour's son, William. William's white shirt, without a coat over it, and the strange ladder, further wove the web. Gos spent five minutes hanging head downward by his jesses, and broke one of his remaining tail feathers at the old hunger trace. The ladder would not reach to the first branch.

Even if I had been able to climb the tree, which I tried to do, I should now have had to saw off practically all its eastward branches, among which the creance was entangled, and the ensuing ruin would almost certainly have dashed the hapless hawk to pieces.

I fetched a seventeen-foot salmon rod, tied some beef to the top ring, and, standing tip-toe, was just able to present it within striking distance. No reaction: or rather, that most exasperating of all his reactions, a silly, chicken-like indecision. William was busy tying two ladders together for me to climb, in what looked a fatal way.

We must have been at it for an hour and a half before I thought of screwing a picture hook through the top ring of the rod. I managed to entangle the jesses with this and to drag him down.

He bated at me when I picked him up, and stood on my glove even more tattered than before, looking at me angrily as if it had been my fault. I said to him: 'There you are, Gos dear, perfectly all right. What a silly little chap you are' — and, with the kindest vocal intonation but with all my heart — 'you bloody little sod.'

Wednesday

There seem to have been two textures working side by side toward the wordless climax of this week. The new, insensate El Dorado of the sparrow-hawk was

124

dictated by apparently opposite states of feeling: the conquest of Gos, now nearly over, had proved too easy and was therefore too difficult. The relaxation from a task hitherto supposed to be practically impossible of accomplishment had left me face to face with its real difficulties, and not strong enough to face them without depression.

Nobody would be an austringer by choice. Nothing could express the weariness of treating with the largest of the short-winged hawks, nothing the dejections around every corner in this, the least facile of the sports. I had gone into it blindfold, I told myself, and now not hated but drooped my wings before it, as Gos had done when he was watched three nights. It was six weeks since I had averted my eyes from the hag-ridden pupils of this lunatic, half a week since he had come on a creance quite perfectly a hundred yards. I had lived with this hawk, its slave, butcher, nursemaid and flunkey. What clothes it wore were made by me, what house it had was swept out and kept sweet by me, what food it ate was killed and eviscerated and hacked into pieces and served by me, what excursions it made were taken on my fist. For six weeks I had thought about it long into the night and risen early to execute my thoughts. I had never raised my voice to it, nor hurt it, nor subjected it to the extreme torture which it deserved. I had gone half bird myself, transferring my love and interest and livelihood into its future, giving hostages to fortune as madly as in marriage and family cares. If the hawk were to die, almost all my present me would die with it. It had treated me for two days as if I were a dangerous and brutal enemy never seen before.

I did not then know that this was a common state of affairs with goshawks, that the best of them were always haunted by moods and mania. Their training was never done, the danger of losing them in the field never absent. But to have worked with incessant benevolence, forethought and assurance: to have worked thus for six weeks in the dark: then to find that, as I supposed, all this work might never have been, that some fault in myself, and a fault which one could not remember or understand, had put the imbecile back in the asylum: it was hard then to do anything but droop the head. At some times one could have joyfully wrung his neck, have with active pleasure and fierce, deep croaks of lustful joy dragged him in half, knocked his head on a gatepost. But today it was only collapse, only loathing and incapacity.

The weariness of life that has no will
To climb the steepening hill:
The sickness of the soul for sleep and to be still.

And then once more the impassioned pygmy fist
Clenched cloudward and defiant;
The pride that would prevail, the doomed
   protagonist
Grappling the ghostly giant.

I took up the burden again, put off the use of the bow net till a more propitious occasion, and re-devoted the whole of my attention to Gos. After a hard day's carrying and working on the creance, together with a reduction of his rations to washed meat, I sat down in the evening to sum up the progress of six weeks. The day had brought the hawk back to normal and I made a list of debits and credits, as Robinson Crusoe did on his island.

He would allow me to stroke his legs, crop, breast and panell. He would travel on my fist while I bicycled, so long as I did not ride fast downhill. He was reasonably good with other traffic on the roads, and with other people: but I could not always promise that he would not bate. He would come a hundred yards on a creance, though not so quickly as he ought to do. He would not allow me to stroke his back or head.

I looked at the list and summed it up. The devil spoke softly in my ear. I could afford to take a day off tomorrow, and try the sparrow-hawks. The trap had been left long enough for them to have become accustomed to its presence.

Thursday

The alarum rang its full hysteria before I woke at four o'clock. Seeing that it was dark, I concluded the alarum to be false and turned over to go to sleep again. In the middle of the turn I got up and began to fumble

127

with my clothes. Somnambulist, a stranger to myself since numbed in all the higher centres, I obeyed the stranger that I had been yesterday, automatically. The heavy, iron-shod boots, with their leather laces: the packet of sandwiches and thermos of coffee which I had put up the night before: the bottle of beer: the dark, high-necked pullover and the dark mackintosh, for it was going to rain: the two live pigeons from the bakehouse: the trout-reel with the strong line, which was going to pull the trap: the sock into which my sparrow-hawk would be thrust head first immediately after capture: the pocketful of maize and oats. A docile Frankenstein, dumb and looming in the dark, I obeyed myself slowly and carefully: shut Brownie in the parlour, stumbled out into the night with one pigeon in my pocket and one sitting sleepily in false jesses on my finger.

Last night the clouds had been curdled high over heaven, and now they had come down to earth. The mist was stratus at ground level and the moon hid her haunted face in diminished power. The monster plodded along methodically, moving with a heavy step, setting down his burdens to fumble with the gates — a moon-touched misty Caliban, trudging his two miles all alone. Nothing woke, no owls, no foxes. Two or three cows rose as he walked between them.

We had made the hide in a place where the Silston people had been cutting wood a month or two before. So my own bits of stick would fade naturally into a background of chips and stacked branches. It was fifteen yards from the bow-net, and all lay as we had left it.

I tied the least well-favoured of the pigeons to its metal loop, stretched the trout line from the trap to the hide (the reel dismaying me — one of the points which had been overlooked — by making its loud clack), scattered some maize round the trap to keep the pigeon occupied, and crawled into the hide. Already it was beginning to be day, and the hawks — later experience made me doubt whether these sounds might not have been those of little owls — were on the wing. I could hear their single inter-answering notes, and they might have seen me. It was for fear of this that I had come so early.

For the next fourteen hours it was necessary to remain in a space less than six feet by three, and to remain in vain. For the last three hours the rain soaked down the neck and ran up the sleeves. It was impossible to see the sky, for the sky would have seen me, and the proximity of the hawks (now definitely not little owls), had to be judged by their mewing: it was impossible to smoke or read or make a noise. I made a long job of my sandwiches, cut myself a little three-masted frigate out of hazel with a penknife, watched the lure. A woodland mouse, lonely as I was and less accustomed to man, came boldly to eat my biscuits, and was soon tugging at one side of the biscuit while I tugged at the other. A wild pigeon lighted on the roof and went off with a clatter when I poked it in the tummy, an innocent and I thought pardonable joke. A solitary hen blackbird ate the maize. The spare pigeon, the one who had confidingly sat upon my finger, consented to make friends with me. I eased its jesses, which were too tight for its feet.

Fourteen hours, and then, soaked to the skin, I made all sound: covered a few poor places in the roof, worked the trap, set and strewed it again with dead leaves, tied a long leash to the sacrificial pigeon, and left him in a tree beside the trap. By this means I hoped that no fox would get at him, since the long leash left him free to perch out of reach, and that the hawks might get accustomed to his presence or even kill him before my next visit, thus learning that there was easy food to be got at this place. I left him with plenty of corn and water, for that day he would be alone, and retied the jesses so that they could not irk his legs.

While I was feeding Gos at home, and feeding the dog, and feeding myself, I thought over the day's work. It seemed to be all conjectural. Perhaps they were not sparrow-hawks: perhaps this was not the way to catch them: perhaps, as foxes were alleged to do, they refrained from killing near home. Certainly, when I performed my next full-dress watch, I should have to go earlier and more silently — no reel this time — for all depended upon my not being seen to enter the hide. Tom had laid me thirty-three to one that I should not make a catch. Hawks could see through a brick wall, said Tom.

Friday

It was so wet, so wet without prospect of ever seeing a decent summer again, that I spent the day indoors with Gos, apart from a visit to the tied pigeon in the wood. The latter seemed to have retained the confused good spirits of tame pigeons.

Gos hated being carried in the rain, and still had to be taught that the bare hand, stroking his head and back, was not an outrage. I decided to teach him this in the kitchen, to the sound of the wireless set, rewarding him after each familiarity with a very small piece of beef. There was one thing which stood to Gos's credit, and that was his genuine love of music. He sat here absolutely entranced, giving the strange box his full attention and watching me as I fiddled with the knobs. It was a beautifully-mannered visit, the eagle sitting courteously in the cottager's ben and sharing his humble entertainment.

I stroked and thought. The whole thing was an unsleeping social problem, a tireless 'What does A do?' which confronted the Columbus at every step. Some days ago, for instance, Gos had been sitting on the bow perch while I was splicing a pole to the handlebar of the bicycle. I had looked round at a sudden noise, to find that he had pounced upon a shrew mouse which had been innocent enough to come within the compass of his leash. He was eating it.

In the time which it took to slip on a gauntlet and walk six paces I had been forced to confront these facts: (*a*) Gos had enjoyed a full crop the night before and might not be hungry enough to learn anything that night if he ate the mouse. (*b*) If I took the mouse away from him it might teach him to 'carry' later on. ('Carrying' was the act by which a trained hawk would go off with the quarry at which he had been successfully flown. Jealous of the food, ill-mannered, suspicious that it was going to be taken from him, he would pick it up in his talons and fly a little further off at each approach of the austringer.) (*c*) But Gos should not associate food with his own, unflown, personal effort, unaided by me.

I had summed it up briefly. I could not stand aside without interference because of (*c*): I could not take the mouse away because of (*b*): and I did not want him to have the mouse because of (*a*). The chain had been forced to break at its weakest link. I had stepped across to him, taken the mouse in my hand, helped him to eat it, and, because really I had been more of a hindrance than a help with such a small morsel, had fetched for him at once, from the meat safe, a small additional piece of rabbit's liver. By this means I hoped I had begun to teach him that, having done his own killing, good would accrue by allowing me to interfere.

Now, recollecting this dilemma as I cautiously stroked the stiff-necked generation, I was amused by a similar problem which occurred to me. When I first bought Gos I had also asked for a merlin which I hoped to fly at larks. A merlin was flown 'at hack'.

That is to say, it was allowed to fly free during its first fortnight, coming into the mews only for its two meals a day. This, of course, applied only to the eyas or nest-taken merlin that was learning to fly, not to the wild adult caught by trap. A merlin was a confiding little creature — it used to be recognized as the lady's hawk — and the one which I had paid for had dropped down beside a goshawk's perch on the very day that she was to be sent to me. The goshawk had killed her.

I wondered now whether the falconer was there at the time, and whether the goshawk was still being trained like Gos. If so, did the falconer assist his own goshawk to eat his own merlin? A nice question.

It was drowsy in the kitchen, with the music and the rain outside. I was stroking a murderer, a savage. Gos knew that might had always been right, that the Vikings slew the last two kings of Northumbria because the Gokstad ship could come so strongly in from sea, that William had cavalry at Hastings as Edward III had archers on the wings at Crecy, that the press barons of the year I was writing about were right about re-armament in spite of the *New Statesman*. It was a sad truth, but we still lived in the Middle Ages. The *New Statesman* was a platonic organ unfortunately, which believed in logic and 'right and wrong' and the world of noun-plus-verb ideas. Hitler and Mussolini, Gos and the irreclaimable villein kestrel, seals that preyed on salmon and salmon that preyed on herrings

133

that preyed on plankton that preyed on something else: these knew that God had given a law in which only one thing was right, the energy to live by blood, and to procreate.

Unfortunate, dark, and immoral goshawk: I had myself been subjected to his brutality. In the beak he was not formidable, but in the talons there was death. He would slay a rabbit in his grip, by merely crushing its skull. Once, when he thought I was going to take his food away from him, he had struck my bare forefinger. It had been a Bank of England apprehension, a painful impotence, a Come-you-here arrest by all-powerful police — I should only have hurt myself horribly by trying to get away, and was already being hurt. He had held the glove with one talon, the bare forefinger with the other, so tightly that only one method of escape had been open to me, and that had been to tear him in half. In the process I should have pulled all the flesh off the finger, like stripping the rubber off an insulated wire. Not from courage, but from necessity, I had stood quiet and unprotesting, speaking to him calmly until he let go.

A homicidal maniac: but now he was enjoying to be stroked. We were again in love.

Saturday

It was another pouring day and the wireless had suddenly died. There was nothing to do until the battery was replaced, and then I would carry Gos in the kitchen, let him listen to his music as before. I walked a mile or two to telephone for the battery, and then thought that I would fill in time, until it arrived, by painting the woodwork in the front-door passage. But note this. In order that Gos should be as comfortable as possible in the meantime, I opened the door of the mews and tied an extra six yards of the tarred twine between the end of his leather leash and the ring of the mews perch. I struck the bow perch into the ground just outside the door. By this arrangement, since he now had about seven yards law in what he was tied by, he could fly out to the bow perch to take the air between the showers or back again to the perch inside the mews when the rain made his feathers uncomfortable. I set to work.

After the passage I thought I would give the kitchen door the coat of blue which it had long needed, but the blue paint lay in a corner of the mews. I went to fetch it, as I had previously fetched the red for the passage. I noticed that the ill-weather and my pre-occupation must have put Gos into one of his moods, for he bated away from me when I came in for the paint, and, being on this long twine, flew right up to the rafters. I paid no particular attention, but went on to look for the paint, while Gos, changing his mind about the rafters, flew out of the door toward the bow perch outside. Evidently he preferred not even to share the room with me today, for I was re-fusing him my full attention. I took up the paint and came out of the door. Gos was not on the perch. I looked round the door. I could not see him.

I cannot remember that my heart stopped beating at any particular time. The blow was stunning, so final after six weeks of unremitting faith that it was tempered to me as being beyond appreciation. It was like death in a way, something too vast to hurt much or even to upset you. I saw the end of the twine lying loose, with no leash tied to it. It had snapped quite clean. Gos had gone.

Gos, in the rain and hurricane, was gone. I did not even know where he was gone. I told my neighbour. I went out with a lure of dead rabbit, walking vaguely all about among the trees and whistling of the Lord, my Shepherd, in a stupefied way. I went from tree to tree in a radius of a hundred yards, but mainly down wind, whistling and trying to think. It was best to be calm: to remember, if possible, what contingent advice, if any, had been given in the books. Failure. My living had depended on writing about him: but now not.

They went downwind: but, on the other hand, the well-head at which he had always been fed on his creance was up wind. I went twice round all these trees. It was noon, the time of dinner.

If one could convey the hopelessness of the task, the hundred thousand trees, the hawk never really manned. I went in to the dinner, thinking that it would be best to have a little break: to be calm: to think gently. Perhaps I should remember some simple instructions in one of the books. With a book open in front of me, I began to eat. But it was impossible. Knowing that my neighbour was going to Buckingham I thought to ask that she would buy me some beef steak as a lure. I went out half fed, tied various parts of my remaining rabbit to the bow perch, in the mews, and on the well-head. Then I stepped over to ask for the steak.

I was standing outside the door when I noticed a rook cawing at a tree. A couple of hundred yards away downwind, he circled the top, cursing. I ran at once, and there was Gos. Confused, obstinate, too wet to fly, he sat on the tip of the topmost branch and radiated indecision.

I stood in the sousing rain, hatless and coatless for half an hour, holding out a piece of liver and a handkerchief as a lure. He would not come.

The tempestuous air came gustily, increasingly, until he was exasperated. Half thinking to come down to me he shook out his wings, but wheeled in a stream of wind which came just at that wrong moment, but swung, but was blown away. I ran, trying to mark him down, but the wet wind went too fast.

Three hours later I was pretty sure of his position, having noticed the cursing of blackbirds, magpies and rooks in a certain quarter, but I could not see him. I came home to think and get help.

At six o'clock I went back to the place at which I had last suspected him, knowing that he would still be there on account of the rain. Hawks did not like to fly when thoroughly wet. William came with me, my present help in time of trouble. I left him at various key places which commanded a wide horizon, going round myself whistling. Quite soon we had marked him at the top of a tree in the middle of the wood. The wood was thick, almost impassable. I went in, leaving William to observe from outside in case the hawk should again swing out of the wood's restricted purview. From then till eight o'clock I knew where he was, all the time. William went back for the tame pigeon and this I now used as lure, in desperation making the poor creature flap its wings and finally fly at the end of a creance. Gos began to stoop at the pigeon, but turned aside as the creance checked it: a series of half-hearted stoops which carried him from tree to tree, like a swing. If only I had gone on with this, I should have had him. But the brutality was too much. I had known this pigeon: it had sat on my finger: I could not bear any longer to cast it in the air and to pluck it down, terrified and exhausted.

The daylight began to fail and I ceased to disturb him. There was another plan, which depended upon marking him to roost in a particular tree. If I could succeed in doing this, I knew that I might go out again at midnight, with rope, ladder, hooked salmon rod, and an electric torch. I should then have an even chance of taking him up, sleepy, dazzled and forgetful of his recent circumstances. Before, I had reckoned the chances as many thousands to one.

I got William, and Graham Wheeler, who had

appeared meanwhile, to go away upon some pretext or other. It was important that the one person who enjoyed some measure of Gos's confidence should be left alone with him while he went to sleep. I did not explain this to the boys.

I stood under the tree, whistling, moving about, accustoming him to the bustle which would later attend my ascent by ladder and rope.

The accursed rottenness of that new twine, my imbecile stupidity in going on using it when I had already been twice warned by breaks, and now the fatal enthusiasm of the young. Graham wanted to be in it, wanted not to miss the fun. He made a pretext for coming back. I cried to him to keep away, but it was too late. A silent, an invisible shadow in the deep twilight, it had sloped away even before I cried. Gos, slanting off the tree at the moment of nightfall, was now definitely untraceable.

My last fifty-fifty chance, my thought and life for six weeks, my lunatic from the Rhine: I searched for him with an electric torch for two more hours, but he was gone.

PART TWO

Sunday

THERE were two days of dejection, of distracted and ineffectual plans, skirring the country round. In them there was little sleep and much walking, while Gos, an enormous and distant kite, sailed in a five-mile radius among a cloud of furious rooks. I saw him sometimes closer than that: the free slave rejoicing. Like the parents of Peter Pan, I left his mews door open, and food tied to his perches: but the pigs got in and ate that. I had an extraordinary feeling as I watched him on his majestic and leisurely circles, a feeling which I had never had before with a wild creature, for I knew what he was thinking. I could distinguish his circumstances a mile away, and forecast his reactions. He looked very happy.

It meant beginning all again, and at a bad season of the year. Hawks were taken from the nest as eyases, to supply the small market which remained for them. They hatched somewhere about June and I could not get an eyas until next year. There was one other way of obtaining a hawk, and that was to get a passage hawk captured on the wing in autumn. They were rare. In the old days when the great falconer's toast could still be drunk (Here's to them that shoot and miss) there had been a village in Holland which lived entirely by its trade in hawks and falcons. It lay at the edge of a heath situated directly on one of the great migratory routes of birds; the heath took its name from the falcons which followed the birds: and this name was given also to the village. Valkenswaard: Falconsheath: you had to speak it aloud to hear its music. There the hereditary families of falconers lay out in their huts to catch the lovely wild birds, with incredible ingenuity and patience, and there a great fair was held, to which the austringers and falconers of principalities and powers resorted for the purchase of adult hawks: often at great prices in the public auction. All was gone. Mollen, the last representative of a noble and ancient trade, had given up catching passage hawks ten years ago: the heath had been broken up, the link broken. The duke's men, the prince's men, the king's men who congregated at the great fair — hawk masters with lean and worried looks who, like the Latham described by David Garnett, would be ready to 'gallop off with an expression of torment on their faces' — they and the hawk-catchers with their centuries of experience in patience and cunning and benevolence (nobody could be a master of hawks without benevolence) and the very *raison d'être* of that village name near Eindhoven: all, like my own Gos, were now gone.

It happened like this in the world. Old things lost their grip and dropped away; not always because they were bad things, but sometimes because the new things were more bad, and stronger.

Meanwhile there remained my lonely problem. No austringer worth his salt would wish to buy a hawk trained by anybody else: eyases were out of season: the passage hawk was a rarity, probably an expensive one beyond my means, and I might get no answers to my inquiries for these creatures in England, Scotland, Holland and Germany. There seemed to be only two things which I could do. One was by some means to catch Gos again, the other was to catch one of the two supposed sparrow-hawks in Three Parks Wood.

I leave out the shifts and expedients of two miserable days, and tell about those things which seemed to concern the future. If Gos did not previously get himself caught in a tree by his jesses, and so hang himself to death after forty-eight hours of dear felicity, I would attempt to establish the route of his daily round. I supposed, like a kestrel, he would have one. If so, I would make a trap for him that consisted only of a dozen feathers and a piece of fishing line — no more twine. I had also begun to make a portable hide by buying an army blanket which, having soaked it, I had planted with grass seed and mustard. If this grew in a satisfactory way, I should be able to lie down under a blanket of grass before my trap. It might work.

The other thing was the question of the sparrow-hawks. I had been up every day to visit the live decoy, to ease his jesses, and to change his food and water. Yesterday I had given him a new high perch from which he would find it difficult to entangle his leash. Today I had found him killed. It had been necessary to look closely at the scene of the tragedy, in order to find out what had killed him. In the first place his leash was not at all entangled, so that it did not seem likely that he had become hitched up at ground level and there killed by a fox. Nor had he been barbarously eaten. Something had plumed his breast carefully and neatly picked the flesh off one leg. He had been eviscerated. All this pointed toward a sort of hawk. There were, on the other hand, disturbing features. The whole head had been eaten, and it looked as if part of the viscera had been. This did not at the time seem to me characteristic of a hawk: I thought that the head being so wholly consumed pointed to a fox or rodent (though the plucking of the breast cancelled this) and the eating of the bowels seemed like a carrion crow. The latter, indeed, especially with the head eaten also — though hawks liked brains — seemed the most probable guess. Whatever the truth, it was worth hoping that it might have been one of the hawks. This being the case, I should go up tomorrow at three in the morning to wait all day with a new pigeon. (I had bought two more, and would be able to spare the friend who sat upon my fist.)

But all the same, nothing would ever be as fine as Gos. The great and good Mr. Gilbert Blaine, whose book I cherished, had confessed to me in a letter that he did not love goshawks. Their crazy and suspicious temperament had alienated him from them, as it had most falconers. Perhaps for this reason, I had loved

Gos. I always loved the unteachable, the untouchable, the underdog. And it had been difficult. For every minute of patience in quarrel my understanding of him and queer affection for his brave and somehow pathetic mania had grown insensibly. I felt lonely without him and caught myself at moments wondering what I ought to be doing now. After all, it had been quite right of him to resist to the last: to recognize, long after a falcon would have given in (you could train two or three falcons in the time of one goshawk), that I was an unnatural force. Why should he, a wild princeling of Teutonic origin, submit to an enforced captivity? He had hated and distrusted me, the intransigent small robber baron. He had had guts to stand up against love so long. I hoped he would snap his jesses safely, the ungovernable barbarian, and live a very long, happy life in the wild world: unless I could catch him again as a partner whom I should never dare to treat as captive. He deserved to be free, but I wanted him still. Love asketh but himself to please, To bind another to his delight, Joys in another's loss of ease, And builds a hell in heaven's despite.

Monday

The passage hawk was said to be what the racehorse was to the hack. Wild, well-kept, sleek, noble: he was the opposite of the dowdy eyas who, having been taken from the nest, had depended on the clumsy mothering of a human being for his diet and toilet.

147

No broken feathers there, no straggling plumage and lumpish, ill-kempt education. He had been educated by nature into perfect poise and sensibility: he, by curved beak and sudden gripe, had learned to be a natural gentleman, an epicure, a confident noble, as we by means of civilization had ceased to learn to be. Certain, inexpressibly clever without mean suspicion, buoyant, whole in mind and body, this was the creature against whose personality I had now to pit my human wits.

Poor Caliban rose from his bed obediently at three o'clock, and sat with his head in his hands on the edge of it. Everything in the little room was white, except the rich iron-rust of the pile carpet and the golden eiderdown and the brown shell pattern of the curtains. Even the dog was red. She lay under the bed as a special concession, cosy, sleepier than her master and under no compulsion to rise so early. She would only be a nuisance and a danger in the hide. The candle made a weak brightness in the room.

He rose at three, but it took the slow, early fingers an hour to dress themselves and to collect their gear. It was raining with cold persistence outside, as the tortoise fingers toiled over the great boots and heavy gaiters. To tie the false jesses on a stupid cock-pigeon took time and time.

But the long walk up to the wood gained by its deliberation. Far down in his silurian mind he was conscious of circumspection, closing the gates silently when he was within half a mile, blessing the dim and blurring rain which warred on the man's side against the violent moonlight of the season. Already a growing wind masked his small noises, blowing away from the wood in his direction. He walked close to the hedge.

They were there at last. When the pigeon was leashed to the centre and the trap in working order, he lay down on a ground-sheet in his hurdle cave, conscious that no bird or beast had been disturbed by his manœuvres. For an hour he went to sleep.

There was an invariable resident population in this small quarter of the wood, and they woke that day in this rotation: rook, blackbird, robin, pigeon, jay. A small and unexciting cast, this slow drama with its prodigious *entr'actes* and Aeschylean chorus was all the interest which I was to have for fourteen hours, framed on a stage a few yards square between the boughs. The west wind, which all day grew and grew, till it had blown away the rain and become a hurricane, made sea-music in the ash-poles to accompany the play. The same wind kept the hawks from working, and I only heard them twice. Even then I may have been mistaken.

The hours of patience showed a single tragic character on the stage all day. A kind of Cassandra, with little or no scope for acting, the pigeon lay flat on its stomach in the middle of the trap. A fat pigeon, a cock pigeon, at home an assertive and talkative pigeon: here it elected to lie on its stomach because its feet were tied. If it had chosen to take one pace backward it could have stood erect, have moved and fed itself in a comfortable little circle: but it preferred to take one pace forward, thus going to the limit of its jesses, which now threw it on its stomach. The tragic action consisted of lying there and looking in various directions at long intervals. Every hour or so one of the other actors would cross the stage aimlessly: a humble dunnock flitting over the trap, or the yeomanly blackbird giving Cassandra a wide berth. At noon the drama reached its climax. A magpie entered shiftily on foot. Reminiscent somehow of Venice, of Italian comedy, this masked and cloaked carnival figure perked gingerly yet prancingly about the stage. Punchinello, Pagliacci, he was doomed to some calamity; meanwhile he strutted about in craven braggadoccio. He was joined by another. A weak sun, blown into brightness by the gale, shone gloriously on the blue sheen of their folded wings. Sinister and pathetic conspirators, with sharp tails for swords under their cloaks, a fresh plot soon entered their weak heads. And for them, but not for me, the scene changed to another part of the wood.

Before I left in the evening I altered the trap a little, so that it pulled more easily, re-thatched the roof of the hide with thicker boughs, tied up a groundsheet as a kind of waterproof ceiling, and made myself a little bench to sit on out of hazel poles. To lie all day in a cramped position, with nothing to do but shiver and watch Cassandra, made one more tired for writing the day-book in the evening than a walk of thirty miles.

I left Cassandra on a long leash like his predecessor, to see what might betide.

Tuesday

The great wind had mauled the trees, combed the grasses and made the woods a multitudinous sea for two days. The year had turned, so early and after such a mockery of summer. Today there had been a touch of north in the wind, who was veering with the sun, and tomorrow we might have fine. But the prime was gone.

All news was of sorrow and disaster. Ploughing along with binoculars in Dante's second circle — it was here that the remorseless wind carried Semiramis and her train, whom lust made sinful, round like cranes — sitting in hedges for a windbreak, or sucking up the sodden rides of Three Parks Wood, this day I had not seen Gos nor either of the spar-hawks. All sorts of possibilities presented themselves. Any one of them might be the single cause, but laid together they presented a picture like this: Gos, on his wide circuit, had come across the smaller hawks and killed or driven them out. He then had himself been driven by the wind far away to the east, and there, caught by his jesses, was hanging to starve and die of apoplexy.

It might have been that the hawks had not liked to move in the wind. Gos might simply have migrated on. Any smaller part of the picture might be the whole.

So, though it was useless to lie out in the hide next day, without knowing that the hawks were there, the tragedy might not be complete. It would be worth fetching a circumbendibus with the binoculars round the Lillingstones, Whittlebury, Silverstone, Biddlesden and Chackmore, or some part of that great circuit. Three Parks Wood ought also to be watched for an hour or so. If the hawks could be placed, it would be worth hiding again on the day after. But they must first be marked down for sure, on a day with less wind.

Cassandra was unharmed when I went to him — his sex did not alter his classical nature. He had tied himself up as much as possible and ended by securing himself in a thicket. I unravelled him, altered his jesses, although with a new loop they had not constricted his legs at all, put him on the trap (but free to reach a perch out of fox's way) and left him to his stupid vigil. These creatures did not afflict one by seeming frightened or aware of their circumstances. Impassive and idiotic scapegoats, they showed nothing but a complacent lunacy.

Then I amused myself by making a new trap for the spar-hawks, outside the wood. This I laid on a tree-stump beside a hedgerow, about four hundred yards away from the wood, in case the creatures (being there after all), did not make a habit of killing actually at home. I thought I had heard them hunting this hedgerow. The trap, although it was the first time I myself had tried to construct it, had been a recognized method of catching hawks under certain circumstances. It was used with a lure the day after losing a hawk. It might or might not be efficacious (provided the hawks were still about), but it was delightful to make and accurate to work.

An iron bar was driven into the ground beside a tree stump and about six short feathers were stuck round the perimeter of the stump. A fishing line was tied to the bar and passed (preferably using the eye of a rabbit wire), in a simple loop round the feathers. It then went on to the hide, for the austringer to pull at

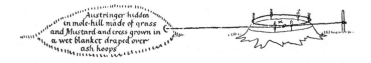

Austringer hidden in mole-hill made of grass and Mustard and cress grown in a wet blanket draped over ash hoops

the critical moment. A lure — in this case, since these were wild spar-hawks, it would have to be a live black-bird tethered — was attached to the tree stump at the place marked with a cross. If the hawk killed and began to eat the lure, I was to pull the fishing line. The loop, sliding up the pliant feathers, would whip into a knot about his legs. The height at which this loop became a knot could be altered by making the attachment to the iron bar higher or lower. I tested it repeatedly by catching my binoculars and finally left it at a height which would, by reckoning, take the hawk below the knee when it was standing on a blackbird.

It was well enough to construct these traps, but it was the watching them for a day of fourteen hours that tested the basic metal of the historian. Every falconer was an historian, a man who had found the hurly-burly of present-day lunacy to be less well done than the savage decency of ages long overpowered, and overpowered because they had not been wicked enough to conquer the wickedness that time had brought to accost them.

Nothing else was worth writing down except that I fell in with a local kestrel and got on close terms with him by means of the binoculars. I was looking at a tree whose upper branches had been killed by the ivy and thinking what an admirable tree this would be for a hawk to sit on. Hawks liked to sit on dead, high branches, because this gave them a good view in all directions. I began to focus the glasses on the top, when a bird anchored himself there. I stared at him long, thinking that he was not a hawk but ought to be. A far way off, he sat with his body inclined forward, where a hawk would have sat upright. As I was approaching he flew again, giving a first chance to observe his flight; and certainly he was a hawk. His body had been inclined forward to breast the wind. I chased him for some time, long enough to be sure of his russet aura, his bachelor habits, and to feel more and more certain that the creatures which I was after in the wood were really sparrow-hawks. The kestrel seems to be most easily distinguished by his lonely peasantry. He, unlike the hunting pair of woodland bandits, went solitary and monastic about his low-flying rounds. Linnaeus, apropos of this, named the chaffinch *coelebs*, because the male flocks separated themselves from the females after the autumn.

Thinking of these flocks, and at a still further remove, I noted that my great namesake of Selborne defined September 15th in his *Naturalist's Calendar* with the few words: 'Ivy fl., starlings congregate.' And so they did. The starlings and felts were already in their congregations, as the rooks were, thus causing many short-sighted shooters to wonder if the second of them were not coveys of partridges. But note the verb he used. Starlings 'congregate'. One could be struck into a kind of muse, thinking that starlings have been upon the face of the earth longer than man has been, and wondering what kind of yearly business is transacted at these moots, so much more ancient than the witangemoot from which we trace our dying human parliaments.

Wednesday

To write something which was of enduring beauty, this was the ambition of every writer: as it was the ambition of the joiner and architect and the constructor of any kind. It was not the beauty but the endurance, for endurance was beautiful. It was also all that we could do. It was a consolation, even a high and positive joy, to make something true: some table, which, sat on, when it was meant only to be eaten off, would not splinter or shatter. It was not for the constructor that the beauty was made, but for the thing itself. He would triumph to know that some contribution had been made: some sort of consoling contribution quite timeless and without relation to his own profit. Sometimes we knew, half tipsy or listening to music, that at the heart of some world there lay a chord to which vibrating gave reality. With its reality there was music and truth and the permanence of good workmanship. To give birth to this, with whatever male travail, was not only all that man could do: it was also all that eclipsed humanity of either sex could do: it was the human contribution to the universe. Absolutely bludgeoned by jazz and mechanical achievement, the artist yearned to discover permanence, some life of happy permanence which he by fixing could create to the satisfaction of after-people who also looked. This was it, as the poets realized, to be a mother of immortal song: to say Yes when it was, and No when it was: to make enduringly true that perhaps quite small occasional table off which subsequent generations could eat, without breaking it down: to help the timeless benevolence which should be that of this lonely and little race: to join the affection which had lasted between William the Conqueror and George VI. Wheelwrights, smiths, farmers, carpenters, and mothers of large families knew this.

It had been a day of profound depression. Too misty at six o'clock for it to be possible to see twenty yards, it was useless to start the circumbendibus in search of Gos before light. The postman had brought a message from Tom that the rooks were making a great to-do in Hoptoft Spinney. Able by then to see two fields ahead, I had set off on a stern chase which lasted till dusk and showed nothing. A little owl, seen for the third time, habited the south side of the wood: the kestrel worked from the east: the sparrow-hawks had definitely left. Gos was lost. Somewhere in the million trees which made a musical shade about his sometime mews, the young Absalom hung by his jesses.

Rooks at this season of the year moved about in enormous throngs, at dawn and sunset, many hundreds together. Trailing along with their loud and prolonged Hurrahs, they introduced my favourite evening quotation from Shakespeare. Night thickens and the crow makes wing to the rooky wood. But notice, as with Gilbert White, the words he used for their flight. 'Makes wing.' How better could be described that laborious and visible manufacture of flight, the wings hoisted and depressed, with which this particular bird made its way through the air? Just as that immortal man beat everybody at everything, so he naturally beat the naturalists at their own game. He took us in his stride.

It was startling to read Shakespeare after a course of falconry. *The Taming of the Shrew* was pure hawk-mastery and must have been a play of enormous vividness to a generation which understood the falcon. It was as if a great dramatist of today were to write a play in which, by subjecting her to the applied laws of tennis, or golf, or cricket (or whatever footling theoretical game might be said to be the public favourite nowadays), a woman were brought under her husband's government. Petruchio tamed his Kate as an austringer did his hawk, and he was conscious of the fact. When you had watched a hawk and regulated its appetite, this kind of speech burst into life:

> Thus have I politicly begun my reign,
> And 'tis my hope to end successfully.
> My falcon now is sharp and passing empty;
> And, till she stoop, she must not be full-gorged,
> For then she never looks upon her lure.
> Another way I have to man my haggard,
> To make her come, and know her keeper's call,
> That is, to watch her, as we watch those kites
> That bate, and beat, and will not be obedient.
> She ate no meat today, nor none shall eat:
> Last night she slept not, nor tonight she shall not.

'Falcon', 'sharp-set', 'stoop', 'full-gorged', 'lure', 'haggard', 'watch', 'man', and 'bate', were technical terms still used, each with a definite meaning. Kate, by the way, sounded very like Kite to me.

And then *Othello*:

> If I do prove her haggard,
> Though that her jesses were my dear heart-strings,
> I'd whistle her off, and let her down the wind
> To prey at fortune.

To one who had just lost his hawk, and seen him whirled away down-wind, this was one of the most devastating oaths in Shakespeare. If I shall prove that she is a wild adult or haggard falcon (i.e. not a virgin, as a nest-taken eyas would be, but one who has already learned her sport before coming into my possession), though the strings of my heart were used to hold her with (as of course they are with all hawks), I would throw her off down-wind to chase after anything she liked. In fact, I would have done with her: intentionally lose her, for falcons must be flown up wind. The awful finality of this gesture of abnegation bloomed for the falconer, to whom the loss of temper in purposely hurling away a hawk (how often I had wished to do it with poor Gos), seemed practically the sin against the Holy Ghost.

Meanwhile the mews stood empty. The pathetic arrangements, the perches, the lock on the door, the spare jesses, all stabbed me when I dared go near. Even the blanket of mustard and cress was painful, for the sparrow-hawks were lost with their more beloved kinsman.

Thursday

Tom, in high good-humour because it was raining on the day when he had to serve at the Agricultural Show, being one of the Committee, and this meant that he had not lost a day after all, because the rain would have stopped his own farm-work anyway, crowed out a greeting to me before I was half way down the passage.

'Well, Mr. White: we've seen your hawk, you know. We tried to get a message to you all yesterday. Mark said he thought he saw him sitting on the clover rick. We were working in the wheat when I saw him come down on the ground. I sent Phil, but he must have gone on a bit. But I saw him myself. I'm sure he was your hawk. I saw his underparts.'. (Here Tom stopped doing up his gaiters, extended his arms, tried to look like a goshawk, and banked over sideways.) 'They were light coloured. He came down so.'

My dear friend now pausing to come down in a graceful side-slip, I doubtfully interjected: 'Are you sure he wasn't a sparrow-hawk?'

'Pshaw,' cried Tom. 'I don't know about that. I don't know what he was, but I'm sure he was your hawk. Certain. Sure. I saw him myself.'

'Did you see his tail?'

'No, I didn't see anything, but I'm certain he was your hawk. His underparts were white.'

'My hawk had five feathers missing from his tail. If you saw his tail you could not have failed to have noticed them. His tail would have looked like this.'

I extended my two hands with the first, second and third fingers of the right hand clenched, at the same time peering anxiously but suspiciously into Tom's face.

'He flew queer,' affirmed Tom, as a concession.

'But you didn't notice his tail?'

'I'm certain,' cried Tom for the last time, intransigently nodding his head, thumping his gaiters, and giving me quelling looks. 'I'm sure. I saw him myself. His underparts were white. He had nothing on his legs. I couldn't see his legs, but he had nothing on them. I'm certain he was your hawk.'

If Tom and Cis were certain of a thing, whatever its contradictions, a lesser man had to be ready to act on their belief. Later in the day Cis had himself pointed out the hawk to Tom, flying after two carrion crows; and Cis could see, catch or kill anything that ran or flew. In my heart I was not yet convinced, for so many rumours made one doubtful. (As an instance, Jack Davis's man was said to have 'seen your hawk, with another one, at his place on Sunday'. This seemed to me almost certainly to refer to the (?) sparrow-hawks driven out from Three Parks Wood.) The whiteness of the underparts in Tom's might equally or better have referred to a kestrel. Also Gos would not have rid himself of his jesses. He might have broken their jointed ends at the swivel, but get them off he could not have done. Also one would have expected the tail to be noticed. Also I had been about since ever I lost him, from dawn to dusk, and for several days now had not seen him. Yet Tom and Cis did not achieve certainty over nothing. I was as certain as they were that they saw a hawk of some sort — or Gos. In either case it seemed worth resuming the hunt. It was a joy.

That day being pouring wet most of the time was

spent in altering a hawk trap. Hawks enjoyed to sit on high, bare branches, and keepers had a habit of setting circular traps, like miniature man-traps of the old days, at the top of poles in their woods. These poles with the traps atop of them used to be erected near the cottage when the old duke preserved the ridings. They were now illegal. I bought one, and spent the day filing off its teeth. I then sewed a felt pad over each of the arms, double in the middle, and bound a thick knot of brass wire at the base of one arm. The wire knot prevented the clutch from closing fully. The padding was thick enough to hold a pencil or one's little finger quite tight, painless but immovable.

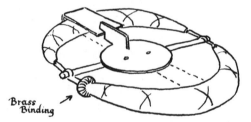

Brass
Binding

(I have left out the spring which actuates the trap, in this picture, because I cannot draw it without confusion)

I thought that this contrivance might be attached to a tree by a pole that could be lowered to release rooks and hoisted again and reset without much trouble. Whether this attachment was ever used with the old hawk-traps I did not know, but it seemed practical if you could find a tree with one segment reasonably free of branches.

One needed two staples, a bit of leather to make the hinge at the bottom, some rope, a pole and the trap.

Regarding these arrangements after many hours of scrubbing with a file, one could say to oneself warmly:

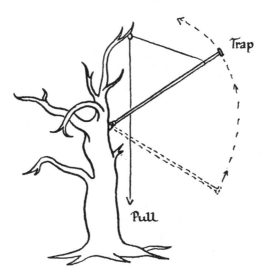

I have created. Indeed, one of the greatest beauties of falconry was that one was allowed to invent things in the first place, and in the second place to play at Red Indians with them, whatever one's age.

I liberated Cassandra from his vigil, feeling that until matters developed more fully he might as well take his ease at home.

Friday

My pride of creation on the previous day had been premature, for I left the finished article on the kitchen table, that Tom might admire its beauties when he got back from the agricultural show. He himself, fired by a similar passion of construction, immediately pulled it to bits, re-created it according to his own ambitions, and erected it with Cis at nine o'clock in the morning before I got there. I, going over at noon, immediately vetoed Tom's improvement in a scene of high suppressed indignation: two rival creators taunting one another as Columbus and Cortez might have done, had they encountered on the peak in Darien. Later I caught Cis alone, secretly asked him to spring the trap which Tom had set, and made a rendezvous for Sunday morning when we should re-set it according to my ideas. Tom had removed the brass wire on the supposition that its brightness would scare the hawks away. This supposition was perhaps true (though I had a suspicion that hawks, like jackdaws, enjoyed shining things) but the removal of the wire allowed the trap to close fast, and this obviously could not be permitted. On Sunday I should tar the wire and replace it. Meanwhile the trap was sprung and could break no hawk's legs.

It had been a day of high hopes. Cis and Mark both swore that they had seen Gos by the clover rick again, and I myself had watched a sparrow-hawk kill at the north-east corner of Three Parks Wood, along the already suspected hedge where I had laid the feather trap. The trap was there, unset or watched, for them to get accustomed to it. I had also watched a kestrel through the binoculars until he obligingly flew right over me. This meant that there were certainly kestrel and other species, possibly goshawk by report, to be taken, if patience and humility would serve, on this little shoot. I thought how proud I should be of myself if I could catch even a passage kestrel, wit against wit, and how he would be sure to teach me something about these fascinating creatures of the air, shy, wild, proud, cunning and fearless, who, consisting almost solely of red hearts and parrots' beaks rowed through the sky by two hard but silent wings (they had the Handley Page slot), were perhaps the most efficient productions of aerial evolution. 'As wild as hawks' we were accustomed to say of the partridges late in the season. It was praise which only a hawk could deserve. It was almost a presumption to match a tame civilization and clumsy fingers against the species: a species which had made itself the nobility of the air since man first strove to make himself the master underneath it. One master against another older one; a worthy enterprise.

The way the sparrow-hawk killed was this. I was lying on the opposite side of the field from the suspected hedge, a good way off, when a bird unknown flashed across the line of sight down the middle of the field. It flew only an inch or two above the surface of the grass. Now I had begun to learn in the past week that if you saw a bird (particularly a hawk, crow or rook) it had already seen you. It was useless suddenly to alter your behaviour — possibly stopping in your tracks and raising your binoculars — for the bird immediately took flight. You had to continue in doing exactly what you had been doing before, allowing the pupils of your eyes a movement which you denied even to your head. In this case I did this, lying motionless in the same position while the bird passed beyond my field of vision. It turned, however, and came back again along the opposite hedge, having soared up on the turn, but now losing height all the time. I could see that it was short-winged at any rate. The French call the short-winged hawks *rameurs* because they row in their flight, a fact which could best be observed as the great trireme of a goshawk came 'in-out'-ing through the air directly toward you on a creance of one hundred yards. The side view of this kind of flight (which the present was) was less striking. The bird appeared to float in so leisurely a manner, gently banking to her prey.

My bird did not drop. Having taken this low grass-flying circuit round her objective (low so as to be hidden from the victim's horizon: he was a humble mouse), she had risen above him when covered by the hedge, and now, planing in and out of the branches which gave shelter to her stalk, softly shutting off her engine, gently holding off stick, came in on him at stalling speed and an angle of $35°$. He squealed twice and thrice, was dead in less than a second by the watch. A minute later the exquisite assassin rose leisurely over the hedge, carrying the body as a city worker carried his attaché case, and sank from view two hundred yards away.

Saturday

The wireless said that it was going to be dull and warm. It poured all day, a slow, windless brutality on a par with what this brutal year had been. A chance and unknown passer-by standing outside Smith's bookshop in the drizzle on Thursday had said that he could remember no summer like it since somewhere about 1890: when they harvested in November, the sheep got the rot, and the hay floated down Buckingham market place. There had been no summer like it since I was sentient. That the wireless was mistaken in its forecast seemed to add a special grievance to the day. I said angrily to everybody I met, more than half a dozen people: 'So this is the day they said was going to be dull and warm!' It was a personal insult.

But on the whole it was a happy day. I constructed out of stout, slim, pliable ash poles, cut green from the wood, the shell or skeleton of the molehill out of which to watch the feather trap when the mustard and grass seed had consented to grow. It weighed five or six pounds as it stood, was constructed as the coracle was constructed by sticking the two ends of the main poles into the ground in their necessary arch and then by weaving the rest about them: and, like the coracle, it

167

could be carried as a carapace conveniently. A man desirous of a portable hide could do worse than provide himself with one of these. The ground-sheet and the growing blanket over one arm, the shell on forehead and back, his luncheon basket or other necessaries in the other hand: theoretically he could get about very well. In practice not, for a blanket of soaking mustard was difficult to fold without damage to the mustard and not light. However, the active and persevering man would be mobile; and too much mobility did more harm than good with birds.

I took the skeleton up to the suspected hedge, leaving it a couple of hundred yards away. I did not want the *resident* hawks which I believed in to associate the locality of the trap with human coming-and-going. It was the residential nature of these hawks which would make them more difficult to catch than the migratory hawks which used to be taken at Valkenswaard. To them the terrain would be known and the least alteration quickly noted. I did not hope for much. If the hurdle cave and the molehill put the airy nobility off, well I should simply have to wait for a month or two, until these engines had become absorbed into the landscape. Tom's odds of thirty-three to one against taking a hawk within three weeks seemed fair. I had little more than a week left, and the mustard would not grow.

At Tom's there was company to tea, but we arrived a little before it. I walked up to the house wondering how cross he would be because I had asked Cis to spring the trap. On the way I noticed that the whole pole had been removed. I looked nervously round the door and asked him how cross he was. Tom's face, perceptibly and rapidly changed, like the chameleon's through four separate expressions: guilt at having interfered with my trap, offended dignity at my having interfered with his, conviction that his was the better, happy forgiveness in return for oblique apology. He immediately and triumphantly stated that the trap had not been sprung by Cis and that they had caught a little owl last night. The padding and filing away of the teeth had prevented the trap from breaking his legs, though it had irked them, and Tom had killed him in the morning. (I was sorry that he had been killed, since I nursed an obscure ambition to attempt the training of an owl as a kind of night-hawk: perhaps this would be possible with a larger species. And also because I thought him the southern owl of Three Parks Wood and thus that I had known him personally.) Tom claimed that the trap, having not broken his stumpy little legs, proved its suitability, even without the brass stop, for the legs of the goshawk. I pointed out that there was a difference between a goshawk and a little owl, the one being five times as big as the other, and that Gos was so valuable that no risks were worth running. After a brief wrangle we proclaimed peace with honour; the company arrived; and the rest of the evening was a symposium of this inimitable host's quite inimitable stories about arson, murder and fire in the surrounding villages for the

On this day I made an extra coracle till dinner. This, a smaller half-section to the skeleton which had been carried up on the day before, was designed to make quite certain of hiding the feet: which I had originally intended to conceal in a gorse bush. I covered it with felt which had been left over from the padding under some carpets, and carried it up in the afternoon.

The larger front end of the inverted boat would be covered first with a ground-sheet and, atop of that, with the blanket of mustard. The smaller end, already stitched over with brown felt, was tucked well under a briar and piled with branches of gorse in an enormous and painful bush. The proprietor having entered the larger end, whose supports were driven into the ground, pulled the movable back end up to him by means of a piece of string, and was to lie perdue.

I fixed and gorse-covered the smaller end, and then came back for Cis, with whom to re-set the spring trap. To this we re-attached the brass wire and tarred it afterward. The pole stood out rather higher than before above the holly tree, and remained a silent vigilant whose uncomplaining day-and-nightly watching might take, by chance, what all the life-cored engines might fail to charm.

Being a Sunday, on which none of the corn could be carried, it was a glorious day. We stood long at nightfall, trying to sum up the chances for the morrow. The high cirro-cumulus, the lower cumulus fairly well set, the reddish sun, the steady barometer, the cows feeding peacefully as one, the open sky, the gossamer on the trees, all seemed to point to a fine day at last. But we could see and hear much too far in the moist and windless air, and the dew before dark was only moderate. On the whole, though fearful now to look for anything good, it looked like fine at last: for Tom and his barley, for me and my vigil in the dripping wood. Going out later in the deep night, I made sure that all would be well. The dew now was heavy and productive, a correct September ground-mist was almost as it ought to be, and, high above, the visible Milky Way almost engulfed the angles of Cassiopeia.

Monday

It had been only irony on the previous day to give us a hopeful sunset. It was the stoic who would survive this summer and winter, the man who expected nothing at all.

After four hours of sleep I went out again into the night, and there was the Milky Way, there Cassiopeia, in the same sky as before. But they had been working while men slept. The enormous dome, sliding imperceptibly on the smooth ball-bearings of the stars, had swung them immovably round the pole. The bear was

172

almost down: the river of heaven now flowed more nearly north and south; Orion, at midnight hardly raised above the eastern rim, now ruled the sky: and ruled it long after the wind had gone to call the sun, after dog, bear and dragon had paled, after the lemon light had wandered weakly up behind the stratus clouds of morning. He stood his ground, the bold and shameless hunter, naked but for his belt.

From seven o'clock onward the blackbirds came to the trap at intervals which varied between fifteen minutes and an hour. There were a pair of them, and they came sometimes together, sometimes alone. By ten o'clock I was trembling with cold, for the heavy dew had drenched me and the sun failed to break through. Four times a bird had been within the circle of the trap, but not at its centre, and I had feared to pull. At the fifth visit, cold, hunger, boredom, sleeplessness and misery made life desperate. The bird was well within the perimeter, but somewhat to one side. Forgetting that the strings were also somewhat to one side, I gave a fearful tug. The trap worked beautifully, but so did the blackbird. Jerked upward by the pull string, which must have been directly between his legs, he left the ground at the same moment as the net did. It knocked him sideways, safe: the leaves strewn on the net leapt up in a fountain; Cassandra, tethered nearby (but, on second thoughts not in the trap, because he would have kept the blackbirds off its centre) flew into the air with a wild cry, reached the end of his leash, stopped suddenly, twisted himself round a bough and hung head downwards flapping his wings. I got up cursing, collected my traps, and left the God-forsaken spot. It was no good staying now.

The weather would drive one to the grave. A weak and windy sun, after a sunless and still morning, had done nothing to dry the dew-drenched barley: and, in the evening, cumulo-nimbus came with a few growls of cold thunder to soak everything afresh with one brief, decisive torrent.

At seven o'clock I went up dead beaten to make the final arrangements of the mustard hide after nightfall, but decided not to watch it on the morrow. Too disheartened by the malevolence of God and moisture, I took the excuse that the trap might just as well stand untenanted for a day, in order that the hawks might get used to it. The danger was that the rabbits might eat the mustard: but I had planted mustard, rather than cress, which grew quicker, because I hoped that the heat of this plant would not attract the creatures.

Tuesday

'In order that the hawks might get used to it.' If there were any hawks, if anything in this world ever went right for anybody. At least the thing would make a very convenient grave, being exactly the right shape and size for that purpose, and the next lot of hawks to nest in Three Parks Wood might well get used to my maggots in it, when I had died of rheumatism and pneumonia in a vain search. If I had been sure that the 'sparrow-hawks' still abode, or that the engine lay on some route frequented by Gos: if even I had been sure on my own evidence that Gos still lived, then no mist nor petty rain nor mean, unholy thunder would in the least particle have deterred a rejoicing patience. But in the worst summer within memory, to sit cramped day long without tobacco (perhaps the most maddening deprivation) in damp and cold and hunger unoccupied, in a place where one was only sure that hawks *had* been, with tools which one had never known to be successful, on an old quest which might from the start have been ridiculous, while all one's letters for help round Europe went not only without help but even without answer: it was bitter work. I saw a sparrow-hawk on Friday, so far as I was able to tell a sparrow-hawk at a distance of two fields. He was not Gos nor a kestrel. From his sandy colour and flight I should have thought him not a little owl. The owl flew bobbing and buoyant, as if, Gilbert White put it, he 'seemed to want ballast': my creature on Friday flew with the true rowing of the short-winged hawks. Yet this was all I had to go upon, an amateur guess backed by the evidence of my ears.

Since Gos escaped there had only been my ears to depend upon for the sparrow-hawks. Except on that Friday I had not seen them with my eyes, and on the Friday it had been a single bird instead of a pair. What reliance could one put upon the word of other people, not living for hawks, and how much reliance on one's own hearing? The call notes of the hunting couple were single cries, singly answered. 'Mew,' cried one, 'Mew,' replied the other. But little owls cried to one another in single notes, and hunted during the day-time, for the country people recognized this phenomenon as a sign of rain. Crouching huddled under four hurdles, the straining ears grew optimist, took the screech-screech of the little owls for the mew-mew of the sparrow-hawks, even pricked themselves for the counter-answered 'tuits', and 'dwees' of linnet, goldfinch, etc. Sometimes a chiff-chaff would almost deceive one for a moment, sounding like two mono-syllabic birds. Any menacing single note, and some of the smallest birds had prodigies of voices, made a mirage in the numbed mind which cowered in the dripping bower. Even that couple seen so many weeks ago chasing each other round a tree, were only guessed to be sparrow-hawks, out of the probable alternative of kestrel and sparrow-hawk: they might have been kites, been falcons, or even *hobbies*. There was no reason why they should not have been rare birds and migratory. They might be gone.

And for these, for guesses (for you had either to watch the trap unseeing and guess, or not watch and hope to guess the better) I toiled at uncertain schemes in a climate of hell: for these rose in agony when revellers were just going to bed, and lay in the dissolv-ing torrent of rain while others worked, or hazarded the labour of a nightly record.

This day I watched blackbirds in a heatless thunder-storm for two hours. I was sure that the scare of yesterday would have driven them away, but watched to prove the certainty, and did not trouble to set the trap. I came away convinced that it would be many weeks before a blackbird visited that net again for grain.

Meanwhile it dewed, and stormed and thundered. What protest could one make against this devilish providence? Nothing, I supposed, except, like Mr. McMahon, to go out and have a shot at the King whom we then professed to love.

Wednesday, Thursday, Friday

One was expending an enormous amount of patience and ingenuity, but nothing seemed to come of it. Perhaps a pigeon was too large a decoy for a sparrow-hawk, whose usual prey when trained was the black-bird. It was no good muddling along like this, in the effort to do everything at once. (Already one was attempting to catch hawks without devoting a pre-liminary week or two to making sure that they were there.) If a blackbird was necessary as a lure, then I had better devote my energies to catching a blackbird before expending them upon catching a hawk. But it hurt to leave the bow-net unused, when, for all one knew, the still unplaced hawks of Three Parks might migrate at any moment.

I determined to make the bow-net automatic, and as efficient as possible, while the quest for blackbirds was carried on. There was a stuffed teal on the mantelpiece, so I converted him into a decoy, in place of the live pigeon which had to be watched. Being stuffed, he did not move about. He was as stationary as the pieces of cheese in a mousetrap, and it was into something very like a moustrap that I converted the bow-net for the time being.

Twig pegged down at one end, The other lightly set under the decoy.

Strong Catapult elastic

This oblation having been offered to fortune — it caught a weasel in the end, but he easily ate his way out, leaving only his footmarks — I set about the capture of the blackbirds. Since it is only illegal to *take* birds with bird lime, but not to manufacture or to advertise it, I can offer the experiences on this subject without fear of the dock. I warmed it, allowed it to spread on a nine-inch square of cardboard, sprinkled the same with maize or tasty-looking hedge fruits, and set it out in places frequented by blackbirds within view of the cottage. It was popular not only with the birds (who would hop about in it, and, standing on one leg, examine their feet with evident satisfaction) but also with the Wheeler pigs, who would eat the whole squares, cardboard and all, as fast as I could lay them down. It was not till some months afterward that I discovered the secret of this product, from a farmer who owned clap-nets, and who seemed on these matters to live a life haunted by visions of the law. The secret was to spread it on straws or any small twigs. These, he informed me, would catch on various parts of the bird, sticking from leg to wing and so forth, until he became too hampered for flight.

Bird lime proving of little value, I constructed a kind of net-sieve, in the garden, on the old-fashioned principle, and led the string to my bedroom window.

There I stuck the shaving mirror at a convenient angle, so that, taking my siesta, I could keep half an eye on the maize and blackberries which were to tempt my blackbirds into captivity. The bedroom was a pleasant change after the hide.

They never came, of course. There was far too much fruit left in other parts of the garden, and in hedgerows unmenaced by strange erections, for any sensible blackbird to take much interest in mine. In the winter it might have worked, but in the late summer it was only a laughing stock.

The pigs came, however, those ubiquitous Wheeler

pigs which had eaten all the gooseberries, black and red currants, windfall apples or plums, and lures tied out for Gos on his perches. They often came into the kitchen to eat the dog's bread and milk. I sometimes feared that they would come upstairs and eat me. They would have done it unconcernedly I suppose, munching away while I tried to drive them off with a stick or something. All the hedges were barricaded with old iron bedsteads, crockery, anything that could be thrown into the breach. They thrust all aside. Eventually they ate the sieve.

But I — lying with one eye on the mirror — and occasionally rushing downstairs to hit a pig with a polo stick, which I kept outside the back door for that purpose — rested for three days and skimmed one eye through Shakespeare.

Astounding genius (it was Sir Walter Raleigh who had written him, mainly while in the tower) his instinct for falconry had been that of a falconer. (Raleigh was fond of hawking.) No amateur could have chosen as an example of incredible portent that 'a falcon towering in her pride of place' (how nobly said!) 'was by a mousing owl' (with what contempt!) 'hawked at and killed'.

Then there was Hamlet's: 'We'll e'en to it like French falconers, fly at anything we see.' Turn it into the modern idiom — 'We'll set about it like French shooters, loose off at any bird we see, at any range' — and the race stood constant from King James's day to our own. It was in Hamlet that the undercurrent was strongest. Probably it was in falconry that Rosencrantz and Guildenstern had amused themselves with the young prince, when they were at the university together. In any case their scenes were maintained by this background of thought: 'if you love me, hold not off', 'your secrecy to the King and Queen moult no feather', 'an aery of children, little eyases', 'afraid of goose quills', and the famous hawk whose counterpart might have been a heron-shaw. Perhaps one of the most terrible images in the whole play was that indignant question to his sometime friends: 'why do you go about to recover the wind of me, as if you would drive me into a toil?' Menaced by the dangers which on all sides he perceived to be in contrivance for him, waiting, as it were, while the plot was woven to beset him, a creature that was being *hunted but not yet attacked*, his mind went to the heron against which two falcons were achieving their deadly spirals. 'Why are you going round and round so cunningly as if you were trying to get above and upwind of me — to the position from which the peregrine makes her sudden and death-dealing stoop?'

Saturday

I spent the day in the grave, a not uncomfortable nor unacceptable fate. Two years before I had passed an evening in a public house with a trained nurse and midwife who had been laying out one of the local farmers who had died. Between the numerous draughts of Guinness which we stood her, this singularly intelligent and communicative spinster had explained in detail the full process of cleaning, trussing, stuffing and laying out a corpse. She had parted from me with the following good wish: 'Well, I 'opes yer stuffs nicely.'

So it was easy enough to arrange oneself with decency and comfort under the hummock of grassy mustard. With room for plenty of play for the elbows, I could have clasped my hands across my chest and held some flowers in them: a practice discouraged by undertakers since it makes the elbows stick out and thus calls for a wider coffin. I lay moistened and miserable, sometimes reading, sometimes sleeping, always listening, from four in the morning until four at night. It was at the latter hour that the decoy pigeon suddenly broke his jesses and flew away. I had made him leather jesses, not liking the string which must always irk their legs a little, and he managed to detach them from the screw which held them to the stump. I rose, like Lazarus, visited the teal trap (unsprung) the spring trap (sprung but empty), and plodded home. Then I made a new trap for the blackbirds.

Providence was very fair on the whole, only at present it delighted to jog me. At five o'clock in the morning, slow-fingered and suffering, I had been tying the pigeon to his screw. He had flapped his wings just at the wrong moment, the jesses had slipped through the hands that were trying to knot them, and off he had flown: taking with him the whole point of rising at this lonely hour. I would have had to walk for sixty minutes to fetch another pigeon, and by then it would have been too light to enter the hide in possible view of the hawks. I had been standing dumb-struck, numbed by this one additional stroke so similar to that with which my lovely Gos had deserted me, when the pigeon had come down in a hedge only a hundred yards away. I had gone over, expecting nothing, and been fortunate enough to find that he had hooked himself up. Then, in the evening, he went for good.

No less than three poachers walked over me that morning, Silston people, in a ride which was generally supposed to be untrodden by the foot of man. Some idea of the forlorn hope in trying to capture a resident hawk was derived from the reflection that each of these poachers, though not resident, must have seen clearly that somebody had been in this lonely place before him, owing to the fact that the rabbits had retreated into the wood. We humans left traces behind, black footsteps in the dew suddenly ceasing at the place where we imagined ourselves to be lying hidden, game disturbed, rooks absent, blackbirds cursing, a noise or a silence, an interruption of the accustomed animal routine all too obvious to the hawk on the dead branch or even to the man in the grave. I could have caught one of the poachers by the foot.

Sunday

I took the round metal trap, which had been sprung on the previous day, up to the woodside hedge in the vicinity of the grave. Climbing a small maple with some effort I contrived to fix it at the top of the pole, and left it to its mechanical watch. The teal trap was still unsprung.

I had learned that traps which needed constant attendance from four or five o'clock in the morning were not worth setting without certain knowledge of the whereabouts of the hawks for which they were set. They might be useful near the eyrie in the spring. When I could catch a blackbird for bait I would give the grave one more day of agony, but after that it would have to be a kind of trap which would spring itself.

The following is the way in which passage hawks used to be taken at Valkenswaard. The falconer possessed a more or less commodious turf dug-out, on the heath, perhaps even with a little stove in it. Beside his dug-out he had at least two traps. From the first trap, which was at the top of a high pole, he could fly a tied pigeon which would be visible for a considerable distance, and which could be pulled back again into the trap at the last moment: from the second, which was at ground level in the centre of his bow-net, he could offer a second victim.

In the Middle Ages they believed, quite a good belief, that everything on land had its counterpart in the sea. The elephant was doubled by the whale, the dog-fish by the dog. In the same way, we might expect a counterpart in the air. At any rate, as there are hounds for foxes and pigs for truffles and setters for grouse, so the grey shrike took particular notice of hawks. The falconer at Valkenswaard had a couple of these birds tethered outside his dug-out.

The birds migrated, the hawks followed the birds to Holland, the shrike set up a cry and pointed, the falconer released his high pigeon, the hawk saw it and hurried to the kill, the trap concealed the decoy once again, the baffled hawk swung round, the second pigeon in the bow net was disclosed, the hawk stooped, and the ingenuity of man had added one more wild grace to the stock of passage hawks which were to be loved all over Europe.

Monday

Poachers, a class of people whose outlook few had troubled to understand, were not without their own grievances. I met one of them cheerfully bicycling up Tofield's Riding with his wife's ornamental plaited basket full of wires. As I was off my own shooting land I could scarcely reproach him for being on Tofield's. In any case he told me a long story, which neither of us believed, about how Musser Tofield had said to him, Charlie my boy (or whatever his name was) them rabbits up agen Three Parks want to be kept down, you know, and so forth. But the interesting

185

thing was the real indignation with which he concluded his remarks on wiring. 'Them wires,' he complained, giving them a look of disgust, 'why nowadays us got to be a watching of 'em the hull night, if us doant want 'em pinched.' It seemed that rabbit snaring was going to the dogs in these decadent times; even a law-abiding poacher could not be left to steal in peace.

Tuesday

My blood had the false feeling that we had turned St. Lucie's day. Life, shrunk to the bed's foot, seemed to be creating itself, seemed in the blank walls of chaos to be discovering an opening, or speck of light. To begin with there was an answer from Germany. 'Dear Sir!' wrote the ordenmeister of the deutscher falkenorden, very fortunately in English, 'I got your letter and thank you for it. I am very sorry that you don't wrote me some days bevor.' (I did wrote him several days bevor, but the letter went astray.) 'Gesterday a had a very bad luck. My half trained passager-gos killed my *second trained passager gos* on the screen perch. Both birds was standing to near. Ma 8 years old very fine and goud female gos Medusaa is still moulting. I don't like to part with her. My onlyst passager female-gos from this year, caught in the beginning from September, is now tame, coming to the fist and beginning to fly rabbits well. I think this bird will also take hares if she has very strong feets. Perhaps I have to art with her later. I will certainly try to get for you a other passager Gos (female). Please are so kind and write me if you like a trained or untrained bird. Female Gosses are much rarer as male-ones.'

I wrote back to this noble and courteous gentleman, who had taken the trouble to write in English and had had the forethought to save me the foreign handwriting by using a typewriter (where I, unable to write German at all, have only poked a little fun at his very triumphant efforts) that a gos of either sex would do, so long as he or she was untrained. But what a devil the goshawk was. My attempt to get a merlin in the spring had ended in the merlin being eaten by a goshawk on the premises of the secretary of the English Hawking Club; my letter for help to Gilbert Blaine had got a reply that there was already a goshawk lost and loose on his own island; and now perhaps the greatest living austringer, who seemed to have trained or at least half-trained a goshawk in three weeks, wrote that his own mews was suffering a bereavement.

The next moment of excitement came when going round my traps in the afternoon. There were two to visit since the bow-net had been rendered automatic, an alteration which I felt shy about and did not expect to work.

The metal trap in the maple was sprung and there was something in it. Setting out I had suddenly felt optimistic and taken along the leather glove, and an old sock, two appurtenances which I had not troubled to carry for a fortnight. Now I had a gun over my arm, pretending that I was really only out to pick up a hare for dinner. When I saw the occupied trap I was several hundred yards away and at a particularly good place for hares. I tried to pay attention to hares, to proceed calmly according to schedule. But it was impossible. The feet made for the trap, not for the long grass. More and more quickly, till finally quite regardless of the fine leveret which got up at fifteen yards, I scurried for a sure view of the pole.

It was a little owl, as usual. The padded trap caught three of these eventually, and one brown owl, before I put it out of action. It was never very safe and one of the little owls dislocated the hock of its leg, so I gave up using it.

PART THREE

SO that was two failures. The winter had adopted what the summer began, wrapped everything in a dull blanket of refusal, opposing to love and interest an impenetrable cotton wool. I had been wrong also, on that very distant day — for failure seemed to make time much longer — when, standing for a few moments in the early morning, I had wondered whether I was well or ill. It had been appendicitis, they now said, and took me away from the staunch cottage among the bare trees, away from a perplexed dog, to a real world of being sick, of people, knives and stitches: and I was then forced, on the day before they cut me up, to refuse a female passage goshawk which Renz Waller had got. It was a sad blow, for the passage hawk could only be taken at the winter or spring migrations, and now there was nothing to do but wait for spring.

There was nothing to do but wait, yet still the now lacerated body opposed its small forces against destiny. Toward the end of January a pair of kestrels were reported roosting in a hovel nearby. A cowman, going out early to bring in the cows and taking with him an electric torch to save himself from puddled gateways, had seen them, had jumped up to the rafters and touched the tail of one before they flew away. I went next day and found their mutes and castings. The latter had beetles' wings in them, with the fur of mice. But the touch had scared them. One never came back, and the other, sleeping suspiciously alone, was too wary for many midnight footsteps in the crunching snow.

The time dragged on, the snow fell and lay, the chimney smoked, and the old oaks which had kept their tattered mantles of brown rags about them made a hissing sound in the north wind. Then the snow-drops came, to be punished with much more snow, and after that, after many seeming years of cruelty and dejection — when the motors were abandoned in snow-drifts, and the farm gateways were foully puddled for acres, and gum-boots sucked in the holding mud, and the rivers and gutters swirled brown and broad and wicked from the unceasing rain — there came the waifs of lambs, and their swelled and wet-sodden mothers got the fluke. More ages passed, while the people themselves shook with a hot influenza or coughed with rasping throats, and then there was a little mild. Hunting had stopped early, after several accidents because of the impossible conditions, but now, and weeks late, there came a burst of dirty Naples yellow on the willows and the various thorns gave out a green and tender effusion. The birds made the still ridings rinse and ring with their music. There were violets and many other small, pretty flowers, unknown to my dumb mind, all over the floors of the woods. The grey squirrels ran angrily between their nests. The wise and charming rooks flew about with twigs in their mouths. The nightingales sang like angels. A pair of very early nightjars were suddenly there at dusk, churring but not yet clapping their wings, and a blessed postcard came from Waller that two goshawks had at last been caught — his only specimens for that spring. One was a haggard-tiercel, the other a female in her first plumage, much damaged. He would send the latter.

The larch trees burned with their lime green as early as any, and the various fruit trees came into leaf and blossom. The bullace which stood outside the bedroom window resumed its leaves, like putting stored furniture back into the old places of an empty house: resumed them exactly, remembering to keep the old arrangement. I had watched them go every morning, wondering whether I should ever be able to live to see them come again, and now they were as if they had never been away, and all that miserable time was a forgotten dream with them. But the trees which stirred me especially were the wild cherries. They had escaped, lived in a feral state. In the orchards the tame cherries stood meekly between hedges, but the geans grew vast and unhelpful to man: free natures, ferocious wood.

It was spring. Coming out blindly like a mole, I found myself in the garden with a spade. The strange, seasonal urge had brought me out into the tangled roots of docks, thistles and nettles, far too late to do any good, but irresistibly and unconsciously. Everywhere the village people were crawling about their allotments, a crowd of hunched Adams in mouldy cloth, slug-hunters who were themselves like slugs, but burning with who knew what vernal fires and ambitions of greenery. I put up rose trellises and plunged in ramblers which were not to survive such treatment until the autumn, erected a dove-cote crooked, made a flower bed and a visit to Woolworth's for seeds, bought a scythe (and luckily dug up half a stone to sharpen it with, while making the flower bed), twined a wisp of wistaria to die round a drainpipe, and bought a dozen geraniums in a moment of nostalgia for the colour of bloom. At the same time I found myself surrounded by a crowd of wild animals, so that all the sheds and outhouses were occupied by something which required to be fed: a pair of young badgers who greedily fought for warm milk and sugar out of a champagne bottle, and nipped my ankles yickering when they were not nipping the rubber teat on the bottle; a colony of wild rabbits and pigeons in the bakehouse; a brown owl whose head moved on ball bearings, utterly wise and exquisitely courteous; young pigeons nuzzling into the fist with their obscene beaks, which they are accustomed to plunge right into their parents' crops, and among them one stock dove's squab, more independent and able to fly more soon.

They were distracted efforts to serve the risen Proserpine, for I had been to Croydon to fetch my second hawk.

It would be tedious to explain all over again how Cully was trained, although with a wild-caught passager each problem was a new one; and it would be premature to write about the other kinds of hawk or

194

falcon which taught me after that. But there are two small matters to finish off the story. I ought to clear up the mystery of these supposed sparrow-hawks, for which I had for so long constructed so many delightful contraptions, and perhaps I ought to end with a kill.

The real raptorial population when Gos escaped — and no subsequent hawk can touch one's heart so deeply as the first one does — nor be remembered so vividly — began to sink into consciousness a year later, when I discovered for certain that my small shoot really did support a family of hobbies. There were several little owls, one kestrel on the west boundary, one kestrel on the east, a sparrow-hawk occasionally visiting from the north (the one which had been seen making a kill), and this family of hobbies in Hoptoft Spinney. It was the hobbies that I had first met, without daring to recognize such a rarity and, soon after Gos escaped, these migrated in the natural course of affairs. Gos himself probably got caught in a tree by his jesses — a poacher whose word was not dependable swore to having seen him hung, but would not take me to the place — and died there. While the amateur was making traps and places to hide in, everything was dying or flying away. Now, nearly two years later, I am sure that the only sane way to catch a haggard, whether sparrow-hawk or hobby, is to walk about with your eyes open until you see one of them making a kill, then to drive him off it, peg it firmly down (with gardener's bast, which looks like dead grass) in the middle of a bow-net or feather trap — one good idea is to tie nooses made out of gut-casts at convenient places on the kill, so that the hawk's feet become entangled — and finally to retreat to a good distance with binoculars. This is probably illegal. Shrikes, and turf huts and pigeons on poles, may have been workable for greater geniuses than ever I can be, in the more propitious atmosphere of Valkenswaard.

Cully was a beautiful beast — though not so lovely as the little dark-checked merlin, Balan, who came after her, and she consented to be trained in two months, in spite of being a passager.

Here, then, for an end of this ancient picture, is the day of our first kill.

Tuesday

I suspected that in very long cross-country races the harrier often felt that he would never reach the end, never have enough in him for the last bit, and that then, when he did reach the end, he found it was quite easy. He could have run on much further, was surprised at his doubts, wished that there were another few miles to go. It was like this with Cully. The excitement, the terror, had come in the times when I was flying her loose — after she had learned to come quickly on the creance — but with a silly ten yards of string attached to one jess. I flew her to the lure more or less loose like this, with the string trailing behind her as an insurance, thinking that if she did ascend to a tree top it would hang down, giving me a chance of recapture. The next frightening step had been to fly her to the lure with no string at all. There had even been a throb of agony when I first flew her absolutely loose at wild game, with no attachment — a throb which was shared by both of us, since Cully, making hardly any effort at the rabbit, immediately sat down on a fence two yards away and looked at her master in amazement.

It was because of her plumage. When they caught her they had broken off half of her tail feathers and nearly all the pinions of her left wing. I had been forced to learn my imping on her, on too much of a major scale, and it had been a bungled job. Now, when she was on the point of beginning her moult, nearly all the bad feathers had gone once more — for there had been no alternative but to use some un-satisfactory buzzard feathers because, being a passager none of her feathers moulted in the previous season could be sent to me by Waller — and she was for that year a truly bedraggled raptor, with no tail to steer by and only one and a half wings for flight. But we were certainly going to make a kill, we were going to kill a wild rabbit, with the hawk flown loose under fair con-ditions, however many times we had to try. Fly powerlessly as she might, poor Cully was going to show me that one triumph, before I set her in the mews to moult.

A blazing day. All the misery of the last summer had made up for itself in this, and the hay was still uncut. For a week now, the austringer had been reduced to carrying Cully in the cool of the evening, walking incessantly from five until ten o'clock, searching for the really easy rabbit which would give the cripple a sporting chance of considering herself 'made'. I had flown her nine times at difficult rabbits already, though unsuccessfully because of her plumage. She was in splendid yarak, which is the proper term for being in flying order, and she sat on the fist with her whole attention fixed on the sport. Her condition was balanced to half an ounce of meat, and I could feel no fear of losing her.

But there were other annoyances — those of co-operation. Cully had learned the preliminary lesson, that she was there to be flown at game, but she had not yet learned to take her cue from me. Since she always saw anything that stirred, two or three seconds before I did, we were generally at cross-purposes. It was bad enough when she flew at something invisible, so that I dared not loose her, but it was worse when an unknown object took her attention just before my own slow eye happened on an eligible quarry. Then I would stand still, seething with indignant impatience, unable to see what she did or to make her see what I did, and the priceless opportunity would slip by. It was like being handcuffed to a moron, I would think bitterly, in a chain gang.

The sun shone, and the evening was before us. We were both, inside ourselves, exhausted and high-strung without knowing it — myself because I had been trying for this culminating rabbit for a week, and feared that I should never get it before the approaching moult, Cully because she felt herself crippled, had missed nine rabbits, and was beginning to be discouraged. We had to get a rabbit today, or the discouragement might break her for ever.

After half an hour of carriage on the fist, Cully roused her feathers for the second time. This was the awaited sign that she was in yarak, that she was in a keen mood and would attend to her business and not give trouble. It was not safe to fly her before she had roused twice — that fluffing rattle of the feathers which showed that she was in a good humour. I pulled out the leash with trembling fingers, slipped off the swivel, and held her now by the jesses only — in fighting dress. We were in the field by what we called the Tree Hovel, making for Tofield's Riding. Cully roused her poor, broken feathers for the third time, at finding herself in trim.

Almost at once, there was the perfect opportunity.

He was a baby rabbit, far too young to be tricky, and we were between him and the hedge. Cully saw him first as usual, and dived like a thunderbolt. I, equally as usual, did not see him at all. So she was checked by the jesses.

She scrambled back to the fist, thwarted and bewildered, and the young bunny, started by her flutter, began to scoot for the hedge. Now I, too, saw him for the first time, cursed myself for stopping her, asked myself whether it was still worth flying her, decided that it was, decided that it was not, noticed that Cully was beginning to make a second onslaught, decided to let her, although I had decided not to, swung my arm — and the giant wings had unleashed themselves. She was off. The rabbit was five yards ahead of her. He was ten yards from the hedge. He was in the ditch. So was Cully. She was panting in a muddle of twigs, gripping furiously at the place where he had been. Her eyes were blazing. She had failed again.

You must read it at the top of your voice, in three seconds, and you will see what it was.

I went up to the hawk humbly, knowing that I had ruined a good chance. I stood over her, while she glared and cursed, held out my glove, said feverishly: 'Come, Cully.' The bird let go of the tuft of grass which she was strangling in her rage, moved a couple of paces, jumped back to the glove with one flap of her wings. Tenth failure.

But I was readier for emergencies now, just as Cully was less ready because she had been checked. Two hundred yards further on, in the same field, a pair of partridges got up at our feet. They were strong, old birds and out of season, but I was too shaken to have any judgment left. I swept the arm on which the hawk sat, upwards, and Cully, taken completely off her guard was in the air. The partridges went like bullets, the maimed wings rowed for six strokes, and then Cully was on the ground. She looked at me confusedly, saying quite plainly, 'What the hell are you at?' and I had to stoop down to take her up by the jesses. That made eleven.

In the dairy ground a full-grown rabbit got up by the brook, with quite a hundred yards to run before he could reach the sanctuary of a hedge. Both man and hawk were wide awake, and the former even had time to cry 'Sha-hou!' a harmless antiquarian habit, which Cully fortunately did not resent. Surely we must have him, cried the very blood in one's veins, surely in a hundred yards! But the old buck jinked in a grass furrow, ran at right angles, and the broken tail could not turn her quick enough. Cully over-shot him, and sat down again with an almost human look of misery.

Poor Cully, I picked her up with hatred in my heart and we continued on our way. Twelve failures in all these miles of stalking, day after day, from five o'clock till ten. One's back ached from stumping so as not to slip with a jar from heel to nape, on furlong after furlong of dry, slippery grass and baked earth. Even Brownie, the red setter of quite charming imbecility, had contrived to catch the second rabbit of her life (and been sick afterwards from remorse) but kill we could not. My head and eyes ached, from trying to see as piercingly as my mate. Even my brain ached, because I had sunk so low in the quest for an easy quarry as to go poaching on a neighbour's land, and you could not ever feel really comfortable when you were poaching.

Cully! Did she see what I saw?

She did not.

We were in Tofield's Riding, the best place of all, and we were against the hedge. Ten yards out from us, directly cut off from the hedge by our position, there was a young rabbit who could not have had a chance. He lay flat in the grass, just a wild eye fixed on mine.

But Cully did not see him. Her attention was on something half a field away to the left, and we were going to lose the ultimate opportunity.

I was too wise to make a sudden movement. I slowed up gently, began raising the hawk-arm gingerly. It rose and rose. She was above my head. The rabbit's eye lay perdue. She would not see.

And then, suddenly, Cully had seen. I felt her murderous feet tighten on the glove. We stood together, staring at the eye motionless. Our veins coalesced, and the blood ran in a circuit through both of us. I could feel Cully's blood wondering whether she was to be checked and whether she could kill despite her feathers: she could feel mine in terror.

'Go then, Cully,' I said. I had not got the heart to cry Sha-hou.

And by God's grace, Cully went.

The moment that the wings flicked out, the rabbit

went too. We were between him and his home, so he had to run toward Three Parks Wood, which was fifty yards away on the other side. He had a start of ten yards and his pursuer was a cripple. As soon as one had flown the hawk one felt as if virtue had gone out of one, as if life was being lived elsewhere. One became a spectator suddenly. It looked as if the rabbit would make the wood.

But he lived on this side. He did not know what sanctuary he would find away from us, and he was determined on breaking back. The ragged wings were after him, were within a yard, and my heart was praying encouragement and advice, begging her to strike now. It was like being an onlooker at an athletic meeting who kicks to help the high-jumper. The talons were within a foot; and the rabbit squatted.

Cully shot over him, tried vainly to stop herself with the half a dozen shattered feathers of her tail, and landed on the empty ground. Her quarry was on his feet at once, streaking straight back to me. Cully ran after him, bounding like a kangaroo. It was horrible to see the creature which ought to be able to fly, running pathetically after him with a leaping gait. But she gained flying-speed, managed to get into the air. I ran, waving at the rabbit, to head him off; could see the bird's yellow eye boiling with fire. The rabbit turned sideways to run round me. She grazed his back. Landed. He turned again, but she turned with him. It was hop, skip, jump. She was there!

I took out my hunting knife and was with them in half a dozen paces. It was a long-bladed sheath-knife, and very sharp. She held him down, quite powerless, with one great talon on his loins and the other on his shoulders, I put the point of my knife between his ears, and pressed downward, pinning the split skull to the ground.

Blood-lust is a word which has got shop-soiled. They have rubbed the nap off it. But split it into its parts, and think of Lust. Real blood-lust is like that.

Well, Cully is safe to moult in her mews. I am in my badger's room, with a big goblet of Venetian glass which was given to me by one of the finest women in the world, for just such an emergency. It is full of champagne, a silly sort of drink, but symbolical and medicinally quite sound. It is a beautiful, beautiful evening, and I go out with the goblet to Cully in her mews. She looks at me with her head on one side, over a crop which is so stuffed with rabbit that she really has to look over the top of it, like a pouter pigeon. The red setter has come too, looking bluish in the moonlight, and stands hopefully, with her head cocked also, between the two maniacs. 'Well Brownie,' I say, raising the goblet politely to the setter, 'we may be mad north-north-west, but when the wind is southerly, at least we can tell a hawk from a hernshaw.'

POSTSCRIPT

P R O V I D E D that one was living in 1619 and training a goshawk according to the principles of the austringer Bert, the whole of Part One is true to life. Falconers do lose their hawks, all too often, and always with such a downward somersault of the heart that it almost suffocates them.

But one was not living in 1619, and it was not until a couple of summers after my first engagement with Gos that I met a living hawk-master among his feather-perfect raptors, watched him at work, and discovered that falconry was a living art. It was not a dead one, something that ended in 1619, but a growing and progressing skill which had developed into something quite different by 1950, and which will continue to develop.

Imagine the Tudor staircase in a country house, with all its coats-of-arms and carved balusters and heraldic griffins: compare it mentally with the chromium staircase in a modern hotel: and you will have imagined the difference between what I had been doing to Gos and what a reasonable austringer would do today.

It is quite unnecessary to 'watch' a hawk in order to man her.

A proper austringer would have set about the

training as follows, whether it was for an eyas or a passager.

First he would have provided himself with a 'block', though a bow-perch is practically as good.

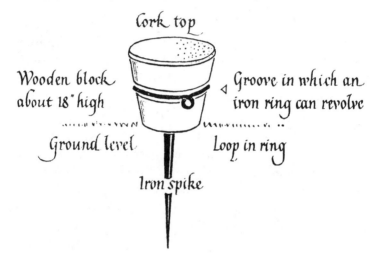

Cork top

Wooden block about 18" high

Groove in which an iron ring can revolve

Ground level

Loop in ring

Iron spike

Having dressed the hawk in her jesses and leash, he would have taken this block to the very most secluded part of his garden, thrust the spike into the ground, and tied the hawk's leash to the loop in the ring with a falconer's knot.

While we are about it, and since it has been mentioned in the body of the text, and since it is a beautiful creature, we may as well have a picture of this knot. It possesses the necessary merit that it can be tied with one hand in ten seconds — falconers only have one hand, because the hawk is always sitting on the other — and it is impregnable.

Well, having tied his goshawk to the block, he would leave her in her privacy, only visiting her once or twice a day to feed her. He would throw down the food beside the block, the exact quantity necessary to keep her in health, and he would go away at once.

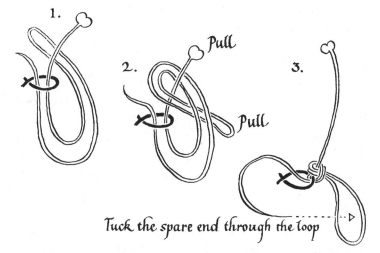

1.

2.

3.

Pull

Pull

Tuck the spare end through the loop

After a few days, he would move her block to a slightly more populous part of the garden, where she might perhaps be passed by the gardener every now and then. He would continue to feed her as before. A few more days, and she would be on a distant edge of the lawn: she would see the traffic at the front and back doors. A few more, and perhaps she would be slap in the middle of the lawn, though the lawnmower would give her a fairly wide berth. Later, people would be allowed to go and look at her, perhaps not too close, and she would have begun to know and anticipate her regular hour for food. She would tolerate her future master, would let him stand by for a little when he brought the meat, and she might even begin to jump toward it before he could set it down. Thus all would pass off pleasantly and easily, imperceptibly and naturally — almost lazily.

I have always noticed that the true maestro gives an impression of leisure and laziness in performing his feats.

From this point he would decrease her rations, would begin to make her jump to him for them, would have her on the creance quite soon, would decrease the gorges severely to the point of real hunger, would discard the creance — some people call it the 'cranes' — and he would be flying a loose hawk without anxiety in about the same time as it took me to start my second watch.

But he would weigh the hawk every day: he would have calculated the amount of food needed to keep her sharp set with such nicety that he had to weigh the meat on a letter balance: and if he took his attention off her stomach for one day, he would be just as likely to lose her as I was.

6.2.51

No doubt it would have been charming to introduce a little fiction later on, in which, one spring morning when I was sitting white-haired at my lonely cottage window, there came a gentle peck on the window-pane, and there, looking sleek and happy, with his new wife peeping shyly at her toes and the cosy crocodile of babies lined up behind them. . . .

Unfortunately those things do not happen in the wild life led by hawks. Nothing is more certain than that Gos entangled his jesses in one of the myriad trees of the Ridings, and there, hanging upside down by the mildewed leathers, his bundle of green bones and ruined feathers may still be swinging in the winter wind.

He would have died of apoplexy, or he may have been shot by a keeper, but it is almost certain that he would not have lived. For it is an odd fact that gos-hawks generally have to be taught to kill. In the natural state, their parents teach them. In captivity, the austringer must.

Except for the shrew-mouse which he killed by himself, if you remember, I had probably not reached that stage with Gos. He would have decided to come back to his perch to avoid starvation, or he would have hung himself, or he would have been destroyed by a human. I can only suppose now that those 'majestic and leisurely circles' of the free and happy Gos on page 143 were either a delusion caused by a lot of distant rooks circling round a lot of distant rooks, sup-posed to be mobbing him, or else they were a lie written in the effort to give the reader of the book which I was then trying to write some sort of happy ending. It is to apologize for that kind of ignorance or deception that I have been allowed these pages of postscript.

As a matter of fact, it was far from easy to turn the day-book into a journal for Parts Two and Three without telling lies, for there was a guilty secret which had to be concealed at all costs. I had to twist and turn the matter about with desire and indecision, and one of the reasons why I eventually threw the whole thing aside for fifteen years was because I did not know how to conceal this secret, was too ignorant to be certain whether it was a secret, and had in fact failed to conceal it.

The secret was the Hobbies. They are among the rarest of all falcons which migrate to breed in England, so rare that one absolutely must not tell anybody about them, and particularly not in print. All the names in my book are real names. Any unscrupulous ornithologist had only to identify the place or me, hang about it with a pair of binoculars at the right season, and then diminish the number of English nesting hobbies by one pair.

I should still be unable to publish about them today,[1] except for the fact that in the Second World War a prodigious aerodrome was built on their door-step, which is now being used by a set of beetle-men who buzz round and round it in motor cars, and the lovely hobbies have cleared off of their own accord.

9.2.51

Falconry is as old as Babylon. It has never been a dead sport, and it does keep on developing. At the present moment it is developing in America, where

[1] Of course I stopped trying to catch them when I realized they were hobbies.

young and enthusiastic and progressive falconers are doing wonders by not fussing. If a good American falconer would come over to Europe and show us how he does things, it would make the old fogies blink.

Falconry is extraordinarily tenacious. To have existed since Babylon, it must have had a regular fount of sap in it. Like ivy, it finds its way around obstacles and keeps growing.

When Pteryphlegia or the Art of Shooting Flying came into fashion, one might have thought that the Purdey would supercede the hawk. But Prince Albert decided to build his Crystal Palace for the Great Exhibition round a tree, and the cocky London sparrows refused to abandon the tree. It was found that the beautiful exhibits in the Great Hall, and the observers too, were getting speckled by the sparrows. Queen Victoria, in despair, sent for the Duke of Wellington. 'Try sparrow-hawks, ma'am,' he said, and she did, and it worked.

Even in the Second World War, the art managed to find a foot-hold. It was discovered that the small birds on airfields were lethal to aircraft, if they happened to collide in the wrong places. A lark could go through a windscreen like a bullet. So the Royal Air Force set up a section of falconers of its own — such an open-minded thing to do, and so typical of that great Force — and it was the business of the Squadron-Leaders of the Falconry Squadron to train hawks and to keep little birds off airfields. The science was officially recognized, and it kept alive.

That arm of the Air Force has now been abolished. No hawk, except possibly the little merlin, can any longer be kept on a meat ration of four ounces a week in England, because, during the moult, they must be maintained from the larder.

The thing will go on in America, and we must console ourselves with that. But what Purdey did not achieve, what Hitler did not achieve, has been achieved now.

10.2.51

'To Attila King of the Huns,' says Aldrovandus, 'the most truculent of men, who used to be called the Scourge of God, the goshawk was such a charmer that he bore it crowned on his badge, his helm and his helmet.' He adds the quotation from Lucan:

His praeter Latias acies, erat impiger Astur.

11.2.51

The thing about being associated with a hawk is that one cannot be slipshod about it. No hawk can be a pet. There is no sentimentality. In a way, it is the psychiatrist's art. One is matching one's mind against another mind with deadly reason and interest. One desires no transference of affection, demands no ignoble homage or gratitude. It is a tonic for the less forthright savagery of the human heart.

Did He who made the Lamb make thee? Well, yes, he did.

12.2.51

When a hawk is flown at game, it must be rewarded for the kill. When a falcon has eaten the heads of about three grouse, she ceases to be sharp-set and therefore becomes unsafe to fly.

So no falconer can indulge in a battue.

If we were able to add up the number of rabbits killed by a free goshawk in one year, and the number killed by a trained one which had to be maintained from the larder during the moult, the numbers would probably be equal. Unlike the shooter who kills his tame pheasants by the thousand, the ferocious austringer is probably not adding to the number of rabbits who would be slain in any case.

13.2.51

By some sport of chance, the nice word 'tiercel' has not cropped up in any part of this book. Among the raptors on the whole, the female is always about one third bigger than the male. So the male is called a tiercel. Gos was one.

14.2.51

There is an old proverb which says: 'When your first wife dies, she makes such a hole in your heart that all the rest slip through.' It is a true one.

Since the days of Gos and Cully, this writer has trained, apart from owls, two merlins, five peregrines, and even been the titular owner for a few brief weeks of a gyr-falcon from Iceland, one of whose siblings was solemnly flown over to Germany in a corrugated-iron aeroplane and presented to General Goering.

Each one of these assassins had his or her own character: they were as individual and different from each other as eight separate anarchists. One remembers them with love and interest. But the chieftain of them all must always be Gos.

The Goshawk, says Aldrovandus, is known as the Bird of Apollo, because he is sacred to the sun. This can only be due to his flaming eye. Looking back through the rather thick mist of fifteen years, I remember him mainly by his armour-plated shins, with the knotted toes ending in their griping scimitars. I wear a beard, and for some reason which I cannot now recall, he once struck me in the chin. I can remember standing, grinning like a wolf, as the blood plied and roped itself in the hairy tangle, while Gos went on with the meal which he was being given. I can remember the feathery 'plus-fours' which covered his upper thighs, and the way in which the muscles there would clench convulsively when he was in his tyranny. He was a Hittite, a worshipper of Moloch. He immolated victims, sacked cities, put virgins and children to the sword. He was never a shabby tiger. He was a Prussian officer in a pickelhaube, flashing a monocle, who sabred civilians when they crossed his path. He would have got on excellently with Attila, the most truculent of men. He was an Egyptian

hieroglyph, a winged bull of Assyria. He was one of
the lunatic dukes or cardinals in the Elizabethan plays
of Webster.

> But Hark! the cry is Astur,
> And Lo! the ranks divide,
> And the Great Lord of Luna
> Comes with his stately stride.